So, You Want to Be Like Christ?
Workbook

Eight Essentials to Get You There

BASED ON THE BOOK BY

CHARLES R. SWINDOLL

Produced in association with CREATIVE MINISTRIES
Insight for Living

W PUBLISHING GROUP™
www.wpublishinggroup.com
A Division of Thomas Nelson, Inc.
www.ThomasNelson.com

So, You Want to Be Like Christ?
Eight Essentials to Get You There

Workbook

Copyright © 2005 by Charles R. Swindoll, Inc.

Original sermons, outlines, charts, and transcripts:
Copyright © and (p) 1996, 2004 by Charles R. Swindoll, Inc.

Published by W Publishing Group, A Division of Thomas Nelson, Inc., Post Office Box 141000, Nashville, Tennessee, 37214.

Published in association with Yates & Yates, LLP, Attorneys and Counselors, Orange, California.

W Publishing Group books may be purchased in bulk for educational, business, fundraising, or sales promotional use. For information, please email SpecialMarkets@ThomasNelson.com.

Scripture quotations identified (AMP) were taken from the *Amplified*® Bible, Copyright © 1954, 1958, 1962, 1964, 1965, 1987 by The Lockman Foundation. Used by permission. (www.lockman.org)

Scripture quotations identified (KJV) are from the King James Version. Public Domain.

Scripture quotations identified (MSG) were taken from THE MESSAGE by Eugene H. Peterson. Copyright © 1993, 1994, 1995, 1996, 2000, 2001, 2002. Used by permission of NavPress Publishing Group. All rights reserved.

An effort has been made to locate sources and obtain permission where necessary for the quotations used in this book. In the event of any unintentional omission, a modification will gladly be incorporated in future printings.

Editorial Staff: Shady Oaks Studio, Bedford, TX 76022
Cover Design: Kirk DouPonce, DogEaredDesign.com
Cover Photo by Stephen Gardner, PixelWorksStudio.com

ISBN 1-4185-0706-7

Printed in the United States of America
05 06 07 08 09 10 VG 6 5 4 3 2 1

FROM THE BIBLE-TEACHING MINISTRY OF CHARLES R. SWINDOLL

Charles R. Swindoll has devoted his life to the clear, practical teaching and application of God's Word and His grace. A pastor at heart, Chuck has served as senior pastor to congregations in Texas, Massachusetts, and California. He currently pastors Stonebriar Community Church in Frisco, Texas, but Chuck's listening audience extends far beyond a local church body. As a leading program in Christian broadcasting, *Insight for Living* airs in major Christian radio markets around the world, reaching people groups in languages they can understand. Chuck's extensive writing ministry has also served the body of Christ worldwide and his leadership as president and now chancellor of Dallas Theological Seminary has helped prepare and equip a new generation for ministry. Chuck and Cynthia, his partner in life and ministry, have four grown children and ten grandchildren.

Based upon the original outlines, charts, and transcripts of Charles R. Swindoll's sermons, the workbook text was developed and written by Michael J. Svigel, creative writer and resource specialist in the Creative Ministries Department of Insight for Living. Michael is a graduate of Dallas Theological Seminary with the Master of Theology degree.

Editor in Chief: Cynthia Swindoll, President
Director: Mark Gaither, Th.M., Dallas Theological Seminary
Theological Editor: Wayne Stiles, Th.M., D.Min., Dallas Theological Seminary
Content Editor: Amy Snedaker, Bachelor of Arts degree in English, Rhodes College
Collaborative material was provided by the Creative Ministries Department.

Contents

A Letter from Chuck

A FEW YEARS AGO, Cynthia and I took a long-overdue journey back to Houston, Texas, visiting places where we once lived, studied, fell in love, and worshiped. We laughed and sighed as we recalled the sights and sounds of a different life, remembered faces almost forgotten, and relived the celebrations and sorrows we had shared. As Houston receded in our rearview mirror, Cynthia and I realized two things: *change is necessary* and *perspective is essential.*

I'm convinced that we all need to do that from time to time. Each of us needs to return to our spiritual roots to reflect on changes that have taken place and to gain fresh perspective. You may need to begin your own journey today. Ask yourself some tough questions: "How have I changed in my life as a follower of Christ? Have I lost my first love? Hit a plateau? Bottomed out? Am I just acting like a Christian, or am I overflowing with deep devotion to my Savior?" You may discover an urgent need to reignite an intimacy with God that has faded to a pile of cooling embers over the years.

But how?

After forty-plus years of ministry I've found there are at least eight essential disciplines that breathe new life into your relationship with God: intimacy, simplicity, silence and solitude, surrender, prayer, humility, self-control, and sacrifice. This workbook is designed to help you cultivate these disciplines, to keep intimacy with God at the core of your soul, and to fan your original love for God so that the distractions of clutter, busyness, and self-centered pursuits have all but smothered. It's my hope that each lesson will give you the right perspective, helping you make several significant changes in your life. Whether you take this journey alone or with others, may God's Spirit make you more like Christ, marked by a deep devotion to the Almighty.

So, you want to be like Christ? Start today!

Chuck Swindoll

Charles R. Swindoll

So, You Want to Use This Workbook?
Here's How!

The *So, You Want to Be Like Christ? Workbook* is specially designed to accommodate small-group study, individual study, or classroom interaction. A brief introduction to its structure will help you get the most from your study.

 "The Heart of the Matter" highlights the main idea of the lesson and summarizes the corresponding chapter in the *So, You Want to Be Like Christ?* book. The lesson itself is composed of three main teaching sections: "You Are Here," "Discovering the Way," and "Starting Your Journey." Take a moment to flip through the first lesson of the workbook and become familiar with these three main sections found in every lesson.

 "You Are Here" includes an introductory paragraph and thought-provoking questions to orient you to the lesson. Groups should plan to spend ten to fifteen minutes on these questions.

 "Discovering the Way" explores the principles of Scripture through observation and interpretation of key passages, demonstrating the relevance of the Bible to modern life. Parallel passages and additional questions supplement the key Scriptures for more in-depth study. Plan about twenty to thirty minutes of group interaction in this section.

"Starting Your Journey" focuses on specific, activity-oriented applications to help you put into practice the principles of the lesson in ways that fit your personality, gifts, and level of spiritual maturity. This section should take between ten and fifteen minutes of group time.

In the workbook's expanded margins, you'll find insightful quotations and helpful notes with suggestions for small-group studies. If you're tackling the material on your own, you can ignore the Leader Helps, but if you're leading a time of group discussion, you'll find some of these hints to be invaluable in your preparation to teach each lesson.

USING THE WORKBOOK FOR SMALL-GROUP STUDY

Designed with the small group in mind, the *So, You Want to Be Like Christ? Workbook* will be most effective when studied by two or more people with a facilitator. The following options are recommended if you're serving as the small group facilitator.

All group members should try to prepare in advance during the week by working through the lessons as described later under "Using the Workbook for Individual Study or Personal Devotions." As the leader, you should take additional steps to supplement your preparation either by reading the corresponding chapter in *So, You Want to Be Like Christ?* or listening to the corresponding sermon. Mastery of the material will build your confidence and competence, and approaching the topic from various perspectives will equip you to freely guide small-group discussion.

You should feel free to mold the lesson according to the needs of your unique group. At a minimum, however, the group should cover the boldfaced questions marked by the group icons in each of the three main sections during your time together. These questions are designed to be covered in forty-five minutes to an hour of teaching time. Each series of discussion questions is marked with Leader Helps. While planning the lesson, you will want to mark additional questions you feel will fit the time allotment, needs, and interests of the group.

During group time, after opening in prayer, lead the group through the lesson you planned in advance. Members may want to share their own answers to the questions, contribute their insights, or steer the discussion in a particular direction that fits the needs of the group. Sometimes group members will want to discuss questions you may have left out of the planned lesson. *Be flexible*, but try to stay on schedule according to the times suggested in the Leader Helps so the group has sufficient time for the final section, "Starting Your Journey," where the application of the lesson begins.

In a group setting, not all questions will be applicable, and the answers to some will be too personal to share. If it's unrealistic to complete an entire lesson during a session, consider continuing where you left off during the next session. The goal is not merely to cover material, but to promote in-depth, personal discussion of the biblical text with a view toward personal response and application. To do this, the group will need to understand the biblical principles and know how to apply them to their lives.

When activities for application are suggested in the text, allow time during the following lesson for group members to report on their experiences. Some will have success stories, others breakthroughs. Some will be frustrated or discouraged. Others will even be bored. This is where the group learns to grow together. Not every type of spiritual discipline comes easily for every type of person. With love for each other, the group members can help one another think creatively and encourage each other to continue on even in the midst of the trials of life. You'll discover that when a group of believers commits to becoming more like Christ, the flesh, the world, and the devil will try to unleash a flood of discouragement and distractions to keep your group from growing. Standing shoulder to shoulder against adversity will result in strength and victory.

USING THE WORKBOOK AS A COMPANION TO THE SERMON SERIES AND BOOK

For the greatest depth of study, this workbook should be used as a companion to the book by Charles R. Swindoll, *So, You Want to Be Like Christ?* (Nashville: W Publishing Group, 2005). Each lesson in the workbook corresponds to the same chapter in the book. The workbook can also be used as a companion to Chuck's eight-part sermon series, So, You Want to Be Like Christ?, available from Insight for Living at www.insight.org.

USING THE WORKBOOK FOR INDIVIDUAL STUDY OR PERSONAL DEVOTIONS

The *So, You Want to Be Like Christ? Workbook* can also be used for individual study. Here's the method we recommend:

- Begin each lesson with prayer, asking God to teach you through His Word and to open your heart to the self-discovery afforded by the questions and text of the workbook. Any discipline must be approached with faith in God, who alone can effect spiritual growth in our lives.

- Have your Bible handy. As you progress through each workbook chapter, you'll be prompted to read relevant sections of Scripture and answer questions related to the topic. You will also want to look up verses noted in parentheses. Remember, this is not a study of the *So, You Want to Be Like Christ?* book. That book, the sermon series, and this workbook are tools for studying the Bible, and everything must be judged according to that inerrant standard.

- As you encounter the workbook questions, approach them wisely and creatively. Not every question will be applicable to each person at all times. If you can't answer a question, continue on in the lesson. Let the Holy Spirit guide you in thinking through the text and its application, using the questions as general guides in your thinking rather than rigid forms to complete.

- Throughout the chapters, you'll find several special features designed to add insight or depth to your study. Use these features to enhance your study and deepen your knowledge of Scripture, history, and theology. An explanation of each feature can be found beginning on page xv.

- As you complete each lesson, close in prayer, asking God to apply the wisdom and principles to your life by His Holy Spirit. Then let go and watch God work! He may bring people and things into your life that will challenge your attitudes and actions. You may discover things about the world and your faith you never realized before. You may find yourself applying the wisdom gleaned from this to your life in ways you never expected. Trust that God will work out His will for you in His way and that His Word will bear fruit.

Whether your particular study group is small or large, laid-back or structured, punctual or leisurely, or something in-between, this workbook will work for you. Whether you use it in a group, for personal study, or in the classroom, we trust it will prove to be an invaluable guide as you seek deeper intimacy with God and growth in godliness.

So, you want to be like Christ? Let's get started!

Special Workbook Features

Lessons are supplemented with a variety of special features to summarize and clarify teaching points or to provide opportunities for more advanced study. Although they are not essential for understanding and applying the principles in the lesson, they will offer valuable nuggets of insight as you work through this material.

GETTING TO THE ROOT

While our English versions of the Scriptures are reliable, studying the original languages can often bring to light nuances of the text that are sometimes missed in translation. This feature explores the meaning of the underlying Hebrew or Greek words or phrases in a particular passage, sometimes providing parallel examples to illuminate the meaning of the inspired text.

DIGGING DEEPER

Various passages in Scripture touch on deeper theological questions or confront modern world-views and philosophies that conflict with a biblical world-view. This feature will help you gain deeper insight into specific theological and practical issues related to the biblical text.

GRAY MATTERS

A study of intimacy with God and spiritual disciplines can lead to profound and practical questions that believers have been struggling with from the beginning and that theologians and scholars still debate today. Use this feature with wisdom and care—some of the issues can be controversial, and all of the issues have been answered in different ways by godly, intelligent believers throughout history. Some groups simply may not be prepared to discuss these issues because of time constraints or level of biblical and theological knowledge. However, for those who use this feature appropriately, it can provide a helpful discussion starter on profound subjects for which there are no easy answers.

Intimacy:
Deepening Our Lives

Intimacy:
Deepening Our Lives

THE HEART OF THE MATTER

Christians can and should cultivate deep, intimate relationships with God, which will result in our becoming more like Christ. Intimacy with God is accomplished through exercising the spiritual disciplines, which are nurtured through a relationship of intimacy with God. Intimacy is therefore both a spiritual discipline in its own right and the goal of all spiritual activity. Along with this lesson, read the Introduction and chapter 1 of *So, You Want to Be Like Christ?*

YOU ARE HERE

We live in a world bent on distracting us from our first love. Noise, clutter, busyness, and affluence woo us away from our faithful Bridegroom, Jesus Christ, who expects exclusive devotion. To make matters worse, many of our churches have become factories of mass production where knowledge acquisition, programs for Christian development, and checklists for measuring our sanctification have evicted the Spirit from spiritual growth. The once-lush paradise that was our Christian life can too easily become a

Leader Help

By the end of this lesson, group members should recognize in their own lives the need to develop Christ-likeness by means of greater intimacy with God. They will be encouraged to make commitments to deepen their lives through practicing the spiritual disciplines.

parched desert, and its dry, lifeless sands threaten to smother our intimacy with God. In this study, we'll discover how intimacy with the Almighty will naturally make us more like Christ.

Leader Help

Help your group become oriented to the topic by listing some of the *traditional* spiritual disciplines: prayer, worship, evangelism, serving, stewardship, fasting, silence, solitude, journaling, study, frugality, chastity, secrecy, sacrifice, celebration, meditation, submission, confession, guidance, and fellowship.

 What two words describe your attitude toward the term *spiritual discipline?*

 What experiences in your life have caused you to view spiritual disciplines this way?

Have you lost your first love? Remember the days when you were a new believer in Jesus Christ, when your love was simple and your devotion pure? Remember when your zeal for Christ was so potent that remaining quiet about Christ among unbelievers was like holding in a secret that was too exciting to keep? In those days prayer was fresh and creative, not stale and rote. Every page of the Bible was like a private orchard, with fruit so ripe it was dropping off the branches. Remember when your worship was consistent, fulfilling, enriching . . . deep? What happened to all of that?

Guess what, churchgoing men and women: religion won't cut it. . . . It is so easy to get religious instead of godly. And all the while, a chilling religion slowly cools our hearts. . . . If the truth were known, many of us would have to say, "I am stagnant, and I have been that way longer than I want to admit."—*So, You Want to Be Like Christ?*

When you were a new believer in Christ, in what types of activities for Christian growth did you engage, and what were your attitudes toward these?

Leader Help
Group members may want to talk about their disappointment with spiritual disciplines. As a way of promoting closer community and greater interaction, be prepared to share ways in which you have personally struggled with spiritual disciplines, if applicable.

What are your attitudes toward these same activities today? Has anything changed?

Leader Help

Try reading each passage aloud, then have several group members relay whatever descriptions come to their minds. You can write these on a board for all to see. If time permits, you may ask the whole group to discuss why these words are appropriate to describe our ideal "first love."

Our attitude toward spiritual disciplines can be like our emotions in a relationship—we may be "on fire" when everything is new, but as familiarity grows, the passion may wane. Read Matthew 22:37–40 and 1 John 4:7–8. What does God say in these passages about the importance of love? Is love optional for the Christian?

Read Revelation 2:1–7. Reflect on the Ephesian Christians who replaced their first love with activities, perseverance, and adherence to proper theology. How can activities—even ones God regards as strengths—sometimes displace a passionate love for Christ today?

Leader Help

If group members have prepared this section in advance, select someone to share personal discoveries for each of the passages. If you are working through this workbook during your meeting, consider breaking into four groups, with each group working with one passage. Then have each group present their answers to the whole group.

Paul wrote his letter to the church in Ephesus about thirty-five years before John wrote Revelation. Read the following passages in Ephesians, and contrast the church in Ephesus during Paul's time with the condition of the same church described in Revelation 2:1–7.

Ephesians 1:15–16

Ephesians 3:17–19

Ephesians 4:14–16

Ephesians 6:23–24

How has your own love for Christ changed during your years as a believer?

So why exercise spiritual disciplines? To know Jesus Christ. They are simply a means by which you come to know Him experientially. By imitating Him, by sharing His experiences, by living life as He lived it, allowing the Holy Spirit to shape you by the disciplines from the inside out, you will become more like Him.—*So, You Want to Be Like Christ?*

DIGGING DEEPER

Views of Sanctification
The doctrine of sanctification or spiritual growth and its relationship to spiritual discipline has been debated for centuries. It is a subject that can quickly become confusing, as distinctions between various traditions are sometimes subtle, sometimes radical. The following books, all by authors who accept the Bible as the inerrant Word of God, will help to introduce you to the various positions on the subject of the spiritual life and the role of disciplines.

1. Dieter, Melvin E., Anthony A. Hoekema, Stanley M. Horton, J. Robertson McQuilkin, and John F. Walvoord. *Five Views on Sanctification.* Grand Rapids, Mich.: Academic Books, Zondervan Publishing House, 1987.

2. Alexander, Donald, ed. *Christian Spirituality: Five Views of Sanctification.* Downers Grove, Ill.: InterVarsity Press, 1988.

3. Foster, Richard J. *Streams of Living Water: Celebrating the Great Traditions of Christian Faith.* San Francisco: HarperSanFrancisco, 1998.

Superficiality is the curse of our age. The doctrine of instant satisfaction is a primary spiritual problem. The desperate need today is not for a greater number of intelligent people, or gifted people, but for deep people.[1]—Richard J. Foster

DISCOVERING THE WAY

If you're like most Christians, you need to step back periodically and evaluate your relationship with the Lord. Sometimes major changes and course corrections are necessary. Other times what you need is a new perspective to fan the glowing embers of intimacy that once kept your heart ablaze late into the night, communing with the Lord and fellowshiping with His people.

> [8]More than that, I count all things to be loss in view of the surpassing value of knowing Christ Jesus my Lord, for whom I have suffered the loss of all things, and count them but rubbish so that I may gain Christ, [9]and may be found in Him, not having a righteousness of my own derived from the Law, but that which is through faith in Christ, the righteousness which comes from God on the basis of faith, [10]that I may know Him and the power of His resurrection and the fellowship of His sufferings, being conformed to His death; [11]in order that I may attain to the resurrection from the dead. (Philippians 3:8–11)

The emphasis of Philippians 3:8–11 is not on Paul's desire to die and be resurrected physically, but to live out *the power* of Christ's resurrection in his personal experience in spiritual growth. Let's study the passage above to see how he expected to see this happen.

In the passage, verse 9 describes Paul's spiritual goal. What is it?

 Verses 10–11 describe the natural fruit Paul expects from reaching his goal. What is it?

 According to verse 8, what does Paul do to achieve his goal described in verse 9?

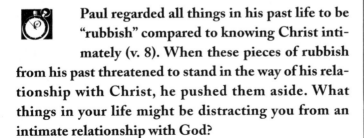 **Paul regarded all things in his past life to be "rubbish" compared to knowing Christ intimately (v. 8). When these pieces of rubbish from his past threatened to stand in the way of his relationship with Christ, he pushed them aside. What things in your life might be distracting you from an intimate relationship with God?**

Leader Help

Members should be encouraged to think about anything (positive or negative) that might distract them from Christ: material things, other priorities, lack of time, "religious duty," personal relationships, and the like. You may need to help by sharing some examples from your own life.

[For my determined purpose is] that I may know Him— that I may progressively become more deeply and intimately acquainted with Him, perceiving and recognizing and understanding [the wonders of His Person] more strongly and more clearly, and that I may in that same way come to know the power outflowing from His resurrection [which it exerts over believers]; and that I may so share His sufferings as to be continually transformed [in spirit into His likeness even] to His death. (Philippians 3:10, AMP)

GETTING TO THE ROOT
Knowing Christ

The word in Philippians 3:8 translated "knowing" is *gnōsis* and corresponds to the verb *ginōskō* in 3:10. These Greek words are used to describe more than just an awareness of information, but an intimate, spiritual, even mystical relationship. One commentator writes this:

> For Paul, the knowledge of Christ Jesus as his Lord meant the intimate communion with Christ that began at his conversion and had been his experience all the years since then. It was not limited to the past . . . but was a growing relationship in which there was blessed enjoyment in the present and the challenge and excitement of increasing comprehension of Christ in personal fellowship.[2]

From *Getting to the Root*, "Knowing Christ" above, do these words accurately describe your own knowledge of Christ? Do you only know propositions *about* Christ, or do you have a personal relationship *with* Christ? Explain the difference from your own experience.

Have you personally received the forgiveness that comes through faith in Jesus Christ? If not, or if you're not sure, read "How to Begin a Relationship with God" on pages 139–142.

Other religions have spiritual disciplines similar to those described in this book. What do you think is the goal of the disciplines in non-Christian religions?

What would the exercise of Christian spiritual disciplines be like apart from salvation?

How does the fact that salvation comes by grace through faith alone influence your desire to exercise the spiritual disciplines?

Because of our twenty-first-century technology and our machine mentality, Christians today often treat the Christian life more like a mechanism of cause and effect than a relationship with the real, living God. In *So, You Want to Be Like Christ?*, intimacy is both a goal of the disciplines and the first discipline. This won't make sense to us if we treat the spiritual life like a destination rather than a dance, or like a conquest rather than a courtship.

When we think about the Christian life as a relationship with the living Savior, the connection between intimacy and the disciplines makes more sense. Let's consider that for a few minutes.

Leader Help
Group members should discuss specific activities they do with friends, family members, or spouses that express their love rather than generalizations that are true of everybody.

What things would you do to express intimacy with a close friend, family member, or spouse? Be specific.

How do these activities also *produce* intimacy?

In your own words, explain how these activities both produce *and* reflect intimacy.

In our spiritual growth, we don't need more religion or more things to do. We need to cultivate intimacy with God characterized by depth. Only then will we

- be equipped to face the trials of life

- be able to live as lights in a spiritually darkened world

- enjoy the good things that our Father has for us

- have true peace, love, and joy in our relationships with others

In short, *we will become more like Christ*, who enjoyed a deep, intimate relationship with the Father.

You may wonder if the goal is to know God or to know Christ, since both terms are used in this book. There is only one God, but in the unity of the Godhead, there are three co-eternal, co-equal persons, who are the same in divinity but unique in role: Father, Son, and Spirit. As we consider this particular issue, we must keep in mind that God the Father and God the Son are not the same person. We come to the Father only through the Son, and to know the Son is to know the Father. Yet there is one God (see John 1:18; 14:6–11).

Intimacy with God must be intentional. It requires discipline. Discipline is training that matures our mental faculties and molds our character. Discipline is self-control gained by Holy Spirit empowered obedience. Most of all, it's the way we get to know Christ intimately. And knowing Him is the first step toward becoming like Him.

Discipline yourself for the purpose of godliness; for bodily discipline is only of little profit, but godliness is profitable for all things, since it holds promise for the present life and also for the life to come. (1 Timothy 4:7–8)

Consider the roles of discipline and commitment as they relate to personal relationships between friends, family members, or spouses. How do discipline and commitment pay off in these relationships? How does neglecting discipline and commitment lead to problems?

According to 1 Timothy 4:7–8, how do we profit from discipline in the Christian life?

 How could your attitude toward spiritual disciplines be soured if you lost focus on the goal?

GETTING TO THE ROOT

Discipline Yourself

The word that is translated "discipline" in 1 Timothy 4:7–8 is *gumnazō*. It's an athletic term that brings to mind the preparation of an athlete conditioning himself for a day of competition.[3] Such a picture suggests challenging, repetitive work involving time and commitment as well as a constant focus on the goal. In the case of Paul's words to Timothy, the goal was *godliness*, another term for Christlikeness.

Read Getting to the Root, *Discipline Yourself,* on page 14. This same word, *gumnazō,* is used in other passages of the New Testament related to growth in godliness. How do the following passages relate discipline or "training" to spiritual growth and maturity?

Hebrews 5:14—"their senses *trained*"

Hebrews 12:11—"those who have been *trained* by it"

Leader Help
You may want to break into two groups. Have each group look up one of these passages, and then share their answers with the group.

GRAY MATTERS
Spiritual Growth: God or Me?

Read Philippians 2:12. Who is responsible for our spiritual growth aacording to this verse?

Read Philippians 2:13. Who is responsible for our spiritual growth according to this verse?

If God is the one who works within each of us to "will and to work," why are we told to "work out" our own salvation? The relationship between our own role of obedience and God's sovereign grace in causing our spiritual growth has puzzled some of the greatest minds of Christianity since the beginning. Unfortunately, the biblical solution isn't as simple as "it's all me," "it's all God," or "it's part me, part God."

Discuss the issue of your obedience and God's grace as it relates to the matter of spiritual disciplines, using some of the following passages to steer your discussion. You may also want to consult your church's confession or doctrinal statement, or use commentaries or theological books that discuss these matters.*

Ephesians 2:8–10

Romans 8:28–30

1 Corinthians 3:6–7

* To research this issue in greater depth, see David and Randall Bassinger, eds., *Predestination and Free Will: Four Views on Divine Sovereignty and Human Freedom* (Downers Grove, Ill.: InterVarsity Press, 1986); and Jerry Bridges, *The Discipline of Grace: God's Role and Our Role in the Pursuit of Holiness* (Colorado Springs, Colo.: NavPress, 1994).

STARTING YOUR JOURNEY

Without intimacy, spiritual disciplines can feel like gears grinding in a machine or gritty sand in a desert. When one to-do list fails to produce results, we may try to change it, make the list longer, or just crumple it up and toss it in the trash. Spiritual discipline without the Spirit is fruitless. That's why we need to trust God to work through the activities of the spiritual disciplines to produce intimacy and promote spiritual growth. It's not about us and our action; it's about God and His grace. On the one hand, we rest in God's promise to complete His work in us (Philippians 1:6); on the other hand, we commit to nurturing the disciplines in our everyday life (1 Timothy 4:7–8).

All of this requires *commitment* based on a firm trust in God to energize both your will and your work to accomplish His good pleasure in your life (Philippians 2:13). So, do you want to be like Christ? Are you ready to take the first step toward a deeper, intimate relationship with God?

Read the following commitment statement:

I know that the world wants to separate me from a deep, intimate relationship with God;

I know that Christlikeness is the will of God for my life; and

I realize that God works through spiritual disciplines to accomplish spiritual growth.

Trusting God to work in me by His Spirit both to will and to do what is necessary for intimacy and Christlikeness, I commit to take

Leader Help

Read this commitment aloud. Discuss how group members can help support each other during the study, especially in regard to the obstacles they listed. Each person in the group may commit to pray for one other person, or to e-mail or call another member as part of a buddy system.

Our great tendency in this age is to increase our speed, to run faster, even in the Christian life. In the process our walk with God stays shallow, and our tank runs low on fumes. Intimacy offers a full tank of fuel that can only be found by pulling up closer to God, which requires taking necessary time and going to the effort to make that happen. . . . Intimacy and discipline work together—and in the process, in a very real way, the means (discipline) leads to the very satisfying end (intimacy).— *So, You Want to Be Like Christ?*

the steps necessary over the next seven lessons to practice spiritual disciplines in whatever way God leads me."

_____   _____

Signature   **Date**

 Is there anything preventing you from signing this commitment right now?

 What obstacles do you foresee that could distract you from keeping this commitment in the future? Think of some specific ways to overcome obstacles that the flesh, the world, or Satan will throw into your path.

Close this lesson in prayer, expressing complete dependence on God, trusting in Him to have His way in your life, and asking for strength to fulfill the commitment. Pray regarding the specific obstacles you foresaw as being distractions. Finally, pray for God's Spirit to work through the spiritual disciplines to make you or your group more like Christ as you enter into a deeper, more intimate relationship with God.

Through this lesson you discovered the need to cultivate a deep, intimate relationship with God and become more like Christ. Along the way, you learned that intimacy with God is a relationship nurtured through spiritual disciplines—active involvement in a relationship with God that's both the result of and the means to intimacy. If you've committed to taking this walk with the Lord, follow through by faithfully completing the following lessons. If you're working in a group or with a partner, come to the next meeting prepared to discuss the results of your work.

Leader Help

Encourage group members to work through lesson 2 on the discipline of simplicity, including the application exercises suggested for uncluttering their minds. They will need to start early in the week in order to have ample time to complete the exercises. The better prepared the group members are, the more benefit they will all receive from the study.

Simplicity:
Uncluttering Our Minds

Simplicity:
Uncluttering Our Minds

THE HEART OF THE MATTER

A complicated, cluttered mind distracts us from the goal of Christlikeness. Simplifying our lives frees up time and eliminates mental distractions, allowing us to focus on the disciplines of godliness and to nurture a deeper intimacy with God. Along with this lesson, read chapter 2 of *So, You Want to Be Like Christ?*

YOU ARE HERE . . .

We live in a veritable red-light district of complications. False teachers poison the simple message of grace with legalism or a health-and-wealth gospel. Certain secular psychologists push aside the human problem of sin and promote positive thinking. And Christians complicate the simplicity of the spiritual life with too many activities, too much work, too much debt, too much everything—leaving little time or energy for God. With our busyness-as-usual lifestyles, many of us barely squeeze five minutes of time for God from our airtight schedules.

How can we pursue deep intimacy with God when

Leader Help

By the end of this lesson, group members should recognize that cluttering our lives with things and activities distracts us from intimacy with God. They should identify ways in which their lives are cluttered and commit to take specific actions toward getting rid of the distractions.

every minute of our day is muddled with the mundane? How can we become more like Christ when our lives are cluttered with chaos and controlled by crises? *We can't.*

 Compare these two work spaces. At which desk—left or right—would you rather

work?
relax?
pray?

Which picture most closely illustrates your personal and public life today?

Leader Help

These are a few concrete expressions of the fruit of the Spirit described in Galatians 5:22–23. You may want to share a personal experience in which you lacked patience, kindness, peace, joy, or some other fruit of the Spirit due to clutter.

How can a cluttered mind affect your ability to give adequate attention to your relationship with Jesus Christ? How, in turn, does that affect your patience with loved ones, politeness to strangers, joy in everyday activities, or calm through stressful situations?

The answer to a cluttered mind is not simply cleaning the desk or organizing your life into large, neat piles. Structuring and organizing can be just as distracting and time consuming as the clutter itself! Organization is not the same as simplicity. Simplicity is having less to manage.

How can our attempts at "getting organized" sometimes add more clutter and distraction than simplicity and clarity?

Leader Help

Focus the discussion on the fact that dedication to neatness and organization can be just as distracting from the important things in life as clutter and chaos. In other words, the "neat freak" doesn't always have a clear advantage.

How can technology actually contribute to the problems of clutter and distraction?

Moving into a new apartment or house is one thing that gives people the opportunity to get rid of the growing clutter that naturally builds over the months and years. Share an experience of getting rid of things you no longer needed but held on to for no good reason. How did it feel to clean those things out?

A man is raised up from the earth by two wings—simplicity and purity. There must be simplicity in his intention and purity in his desires. Simplicity leads to God, purity embraces and enjoys Him.[1]—Thomas à Kempis

Describe the feeling of moving into a new home or office with less clutter.

Clutter is the enemy of simplicity. A cluttered desk can often indicate a cluttered life and mind. There's a feeling of freedom, clarity, and freshness that comes from moving into a new home or office, cleaning out your garage, or finally having that yard sale you keep talking about. The same thing is true when applied to our minds. An inherent stress is produced by the chaos and muddle that somehow naturally accumulate in our lives.

So, you want to know what a cluttered mind is like? Here are five simple steps that'll get you there:

1. Say yes every time somebody asks you to do something.

2. Don't plan any time for leisure and rejuvenation.

3. Don't be satisfied with your accomplishments—always keep moving!

4. Max out your credit cards beyond what you can repay.

5. Acquire all the latest and best technology to *simplify* your life.

Of the five steps listed, which have you most often taken? What have been the results?

DISCOVERING THE WAY

Though he faced imprisonment, beatings, stoning, shipwrecks, and attacks by wild beasts (see 2 Corinthians 11:23–28), one of the apostle Paul's greatest fears was that those he led to Christ would be distracted from their simple devotion to the Savior.

²For I am jealous for you with a godly jealousy; for I betrothed you to one husband, so that to Christ I might present you as a pure virgin. ³But I am afraid that, as the serpent deceived Eve by his craftiness, *your minds will be led astray from the simplicity and purity of devotion to Christ.* ⁴For if one comes and preaches another Jesus whom we have not preached, or you receive a different spirit which you have not received, or a different gospel which you have not accepted, you bear this beautifully. (2 Corinthians 11:2–4, emphasis added)

 In the passage above, circle the places where Jesus Christ is mentioned.

In order for intimacy with the Almighty to become our determined purpose, we will have to make some major changes. That process begins with an honest assessment of what stands in our way. The first and most obvious challenges we face are the enormous complications of this century and the resulting clutter they produce in our minds. —*So, You Want to Be Like Christ?*

What type of intimate relationship did the passage use to describe the believers' devotion to Christ?

 As with a marriage partner, we should have eyes only for Christ. What is Paul's fear in this passage?

 From the passage, what three things distracted Paul's readers from the simplicity of their devotion to Christ?

 In what ways can the following things and activities be used to lead us into a more intimate relationship with Christ?

1. Entertainment, leisure, and possessions
2. Prayer, devotions, and Bible reading
3. Work, ministry, and education
4. Family, friends, and other relationships

In what ways can these same things distract us from a simple, pure devotion to Christ?

The desire for greater theological knowledge (as good as that is) has supplanted the simple call to know Him intimately . . . in the power of His resurrection and in sharing His suffering. The simple message that Jesus proclaimed doesn't require a giant theological intellect in order to receive it and implement it. If generations of illiterate peasants throughout the centuries before us could do it, so can we—as long as we aren't seduced by the contemporary "enlightenment" surrounding us, enticing us to abandon what God has made simple.
—*So, You Want to Be Like Christ?*

 Which of these is most likely to become more of a distraction than a blessing to you personally?

Read Ephesians 5:25–32. Why do you think Paul used this intimate illustration when talking about our relationship with Christ?

When it comes to your spouse, close friend, or family member, what kinds of things can distract you from simple devotion to them? Put another way, what clutters a healthy relationship?

In 2 Corinthians 11:2–4, Paul used Satan's deception of Eve away from God as an illustration of believers' deception away from the simplicity and purity of devotion to Christ. It's interesting to see how Satan cluttered the mind of Eve and complicated the simple command of God. In the same way, the Christian life can be cluttered with complexity, and believers can be led astray from the simplicity of the faith.

Genesis 2 retells the story of the creation of Adam and Eve in greater detail. We are told that before the creation of Eve, God gave Adam one simple command in Genesis 2:16–17. What was it?

How did Eve's response to Satan in Genesis 3:2–3 reveal that her understanding of God's simple command had become cluttered with additional rules? (Hint: compare 2:16–17.)

How do you think this cluttering of the simple command may have contributed to Eve's susceptibility to being deceived and to her downfall?

And now I'm afraid that exactly as the Snake seduced Eve with his smooth patter, you are being lured away from the simple purity of your love for Christ. (2 Corinthians 11:4 MSG)

Read the following passages and note what things (clutter) can intrude on a person's understanding of the simple gospel or distract him or her from the simplicity of devotion to Christ.

Mark 4:18–19

Luke 10:38–42

Luke 12:15–21

Luke 12:22–31

Which of these is most convicting to you? Why?

According to Luke 12:31–32, what is God's perspective when it comes to our priorities?

GETTING TO THE ROOT
Simplicity

In 2 Corinthians 11:3, the Greek word for "simple," *haplotēs,* means "noble simplicity" or "single-ness of heart."[2] Paul wanted believers to focus their minds on Christ, without external or internal distractions.

I'm not worried that a false gospel will carry us away but that our simple devotion to Christ will be lost among the clutter. That we'll be consumed by complication—trivial distractions that swirl around in our minds and blow us randomly about so that at the end of our lives, we may as well have pursued heresy. —*So, You Want to Be Like Christ?*

STARTING YOUR JOURNEY

In Paul's day the major distractions were false teachers, legalistic additions to the gospel, and counterfeit christs. In our day Satan doesn't need to distract us from the real Messiah with a charlatan or from the true Bible with a forgery. In our hectic schedules most of us don't have time for *any-thing* spiritual—whether it's from the devil or from God!

Beginning your journey of intimacy with God requires *time*—and time is a rare commodity these days. The solution to our mental distractedness and to our cluttered personal and public lives is to *simplify*. But don't fret! This isn't another task to heap on top of an already mile-high schedule. It's a *simplification of your schedule* so you'll have more time for the important things. This doesn't always mean getting rid of the bad and replacing it with good. Often it means getting rid of some good to make room for God's best.

Through the discipline of simplicity you'll be left with *more* time, not less. Simplifying is freeing, not enslaving. It's a discipline because it's not easy to do. And, because this discipline is an exercise in subtraction, the fruit of it is additional room—a margin in which to enjoy a long-lasting, satisfying, rewarding, *intimate* relationship with God.

Let's revisit the five steps to a cluttered mind mentioned on page 26. Honestly assess your life as you circle answers to the statements below.

I say no enough to keep from being overly committed.
True   Sometimes True   False

I maintain a good balance between work and leisure time.
True   Sometimes True   False

I enjoy appropriate satisfaction in my accomplishments.
True   Sometimes True   False

I have spending and debt under control.
True   Sometimes True   False

Technology simplifies my life rather than complicates it.
True   Sometimes True   False

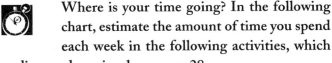
Where is your time going? In the following chart, estimate the amount of time you spend each week in the following activities, which we discussed previously on page 28:

1. Entertainment, leisure and possessions—including watching television, dining out, maintaining your house, lawn, or other "stuff."

_____hours per week

Look at the example Jesus gave us. When He came to the end of His earthly ministry, though only thirty-three years old, He said boldly, "I glorified You on the earth, having accomplished the work which You have given Me to do" (John 17:4). That's an uncluttered life. . . . Jesus deliberately limited His itinerary. He kept His ministry simple. —*So, You Want to Be Like Christ?*

2. Prayer, devotions, and Bible reading—including time with God alone and with others.

_____hours per week

3. Work, ministry, and education—including activities at home, church, and school.

_____hours per week

4. Family and friends—including family time and other social activities.

_____hours per week

Just like adjusting a financial budget, you can adjust your time budget. For each area, ask these important questions:

Is there a creative way to cut back on this time, even if it's only by an hour or half an hour?

Am I spending time doing this because I *have* to or because I *want* to?

Is this activity really necessary?

Am I spending a disproportionate amount of time on this?

Am I spending too little time on this?

What is an appropriate amount of time for this?

Beside the areas you feel your time spent is excessive, write the amount of time you could reasonably cut each week. *Make a goal of cutting about two hours per week from your schedule of activities.* Resist the urge to fill your newfound free time with other activities. We will discuss what to do with it later. For now, just try to do nothing. Really. Begin taking these steps *today*. If you don't start now, you never will.

Consider one of the following activities for simplifying your life. Check the box you choose, or come up with your own simplifying activity.

❑ Things have a tendency to accumulate. If your home or work environment is physically cluttered, set aside time this week to simplify. Resist the urge to just re-organize—select things you can give or throw away. If you haven't used something for months and its usefulness seems out of date, get rid of it. Keep track of what you got rid of below:

❑ If your life is cluttered with too many responsibilities to which you have said yes, it may be time to start saying no, or even to graciously transfer responsibilities for which you unwisely said yes (compare Luke 14:26–32). Discipleship requires discipline, and discipline takes time. What commitments are you maintaining that are taking time from pursuing intimacy with God? Select one, then pray about whether this is something the Lord wants you to continue. Seek the counsel of others about how you can cut back on your commitments.

Leader Help

It might be fun to encourage group members with a good-natured contest to see who can get rid of the most clutter during the next week. You could provide a reward for the person you judge to have uncluttered their lives the most.

Leader Help

The Bible takes vows and commitments seriously, so it's unwise to drop responsibilities lightly or to use the discipline of simplicity as an excuse to get rid of something for selfish reasons. Prayer, counsel, and wise decision making are key.

❏ If dining out, debt, spending, or entertainment is consuming too much time, energy, and resources, take action now. What activity from the four areas above would you identify as most *excessively* time consuming? Commit to cutting back or eliminating this activity beginning today. Since our lives are not lived in a vacuum, someone will likely be affected by your decision. Who is that person? What can you do to clear up any misconceptions, create a support system for yourself, or help ease this transition?

Leader Help

If your group is working through lessons together during group time, encourage the members, as part of their original commitment, to complete the exercises for this lesson early in the following week if they haven't already done so, then begin preparing for lesson 3. Some of the activities suggested for lesson 3 will take some time, and the group members will get much more benefit from the study by working ahead.

Through this lesson you hopefully surfaced some things that have cluttered your life, complicated your Christian walk, and distracted you from a single-minded goal of Christlikeness. Simplifying your life will free up time and eliminate mental distractions, allowing you to focus on nurturing a deeper intimacy with God. Before you begin the next lesson, take the steps suggested in this lesson to unclutter your life—and your mind. Unless you do this, the distractions of this world will frustrate your commitment to Christlikeness. So, you want to be like Christ? Simplify.

Silence and Solitude:
Slowing Our Pace

Silence and Solitude:
Slowing Our Pace

THE HEART OF THE MATTER

In our fast-paced, busy world, one of the most difficult disciplines to exercise is silence and solitude. However, this discipline is necessary to focus our full attention on God and to receive spiritual nourishment from His Spirit. Yet the Holy Spirit speaks in ways that noisy crowds can often drown out. Following Christ's example of silence and solitude prepares us to hear God's "noiseless voice" as He ministers the gifts of rest, clarity, and peace in a wearying, confusing, and tumultuous world. Along with this lesson, read chapter 3 of *So, You Want to Be Like Christ?*

YOU ARE HERE . . .

Farmers know the importance of letting land lie fallow, that is, allowing tilled soil to rest unseeded for a season. Fallow soil replenishes nutrients for producing a greater crop in the future. Similarly, all of us need *physical* rest and nourishment or we'll be no good to anybody. We also need *spiritual* rest and replenishment. Ecclesiastes 10:10 says, "If the axe is dull and he does not sharpen its edge, then he must exert more strength. Wisdom has the advantage of giving success."

Leader Help

By the end of this lesson, group members should recognize that—like Christ—they require not only physical but also spiritual rest and nourishment through the deliberate discipline of silence and solitude. Members should select practical steps toward discovering their personal manner of silence and solitude.

Leader Help

Before opening in prayer, ask someone to share how they put simplicity into action over the previous week. Encourage group members to continue simplifying their lives.

Just as taking time to sharpen your physical tools will make you more effective in work, taking time to sharpen your spiritual tools will lead to success. Jesus also taught the need for spiritual nourishment when He responded to Satan's temptation to turn the stones into bread: "Man shall not live on bread alone, but on every word that proceeds out of the mouth of God" (Matthew 4:4). And we recall from lesson 1 Paul's admonition to focus not merely on physical exercise and fitness but on the spiritual discipline of godliness (1 Timothy 4:8).

 How do you give your body rest and refreshment?

 What do you do to cultivate spiritual rest and refreshment?

 Name three people in your life who are looking to you for spiritual nourishment.

Just as our physical bodies need rest, so do our spirits. Silence and solitude are two means by which we acquire clarity of mind and spirit, listen to the silent voice of God, and sit peacefully in His presence. It's not pagan magic; it's not New Age mysticism; it's not psychological manipulation. It's clearing away the mental static and allowing the Spirit of God to speak silently to your soul, to recharge and refresh your spirit, to equip your mind with the peace and patience needed to live in a noisy and frantic world.

 Do you picture your life more as a leisurely stroll through the countryside or as a rollercoaster ride through a carnival? What about your life makes you see it this way?

 Given your circumstances, how do silence and solitude sound to you today? (Check one.)

_____   Like a waste of time

_____   Like a luxury I can't afford

_____   Like a reasonable option

_____   Like an absolute necessity

In truth, some of you reading this are on the ragged edge because you are continually in motion, constantly in the presence of needs and people and demands, expectations, children pulling at you, spouse needing support, friends wanting help, groups looking for a volunteer, schedules, making plans, attending events. You can't remember the last time you were absolutely alone, sitting—or better, kneeling—in silence. You've lost perspective and you're going to come apart. —*So, You Want to Be Like Christ?*

Leader Help

After the group sits for two minutes in silence, ask if this was the most silence they have had in the past week, month, or year. This should illustrate the lack of deliberate silence in their lives.

 DISCOVERING THE WAY...

Silence can sometimes speak louder than words, and solitude can bring greater fellowship than a crowd of close friends. These strange paradoxes are difficult to explain to people who haven't experienced them. Silence and solitude require us to sit quietly and exclusively in the presence of the living God, accepting His sovereign control and protection no matter what chaos is unleashed around us. Psalm 46:10 says it well: "Be still and know that I am God" (KJV). In the midst of danger, turmoil, and disaster, God tells us, "Cease!" It's in these moments of stillness, cessation of activity, and withdrawal from the storm that God ministers to our spirits.

In 1 Kings 19 Elijah ran for his life from the evil Jezebel, who sought to kill him. Fleeing into the wilderness, he was so distressed he asked the Lord to take his life (v. 4). At that time an angel appeared and provided food for his physical needs (vv. 5–8). When Elijah was at his lowest point, God came to him in a most unexpected way: not in a whirlwind, an earthquake, or a raging fire. Instead God spoke in what the Hebrew text calls a *qol dimamah daqah*—"a quiet sound of silence" (v. 12).

 Set a timer and sit in silence before God for two whole minutes. (This is not a time for prayer or for mental gymnastics, but just for silence.)

How did these two minutes of silence make you feel? Uncomfortable? Anxious? Bored?

 What kinds of things did you think about during these two minutes?

 In the lack of external noise, did you still experience mental "noise"?

The purpose of silence is not to receive extrabiblical instructions or secret messages from God. Yet somehow in the crucible of silence the Holy Spirit boils the truth we receive from Scripture down to its essence, reveals specific insights that are pertinent, and then applies them to our most perplexing problems and our most stubborn misconceptions. — *So, You Want to Be Like Christ?*

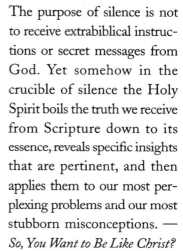 What external and internal challenges would you face if you were asked to sit silently before God for fifteen minutes?

There's one thing about silence and solitude that's true of most of us: we don't have much of it. But do we really need it? To answer this question, let's take a look at the example of Christ and His disciples.

GETTING TO THE ROOT
Secluded Place

Mark 1:35 says Jesus went to a "secluded place." The Greek word for "secluded" is *erēmos*. It means "abandoned, empty, desolate."[1] It was a place where there were no people or distractions—the perfect time and place for silence and solitude.

---

[35]In the early morning, while it was still dark, Jesus got up, left the house, and went away to a secluded place, and was praying there. [36]Simon and his companions searched for Him; [37]they found Him, and said to Him, "Everyone is looking for You." [38]He said to them, "Let us go somewhere else to the towns nearby, so that I may preach there also; for that is what I came for." (Mark 1:35–38)

 As Jesus sought seclusion, what is significant about the timing He chose? List as many observations as you can.

 Given your own schedule, what time of the day makes the most sense for a period of solitude?

[30]The apostles gathered together with Jesus; and they reported to Him all that they had done and taught. [31]And He said to them, "Come away by yourselves to a secluded place and rest a while." (For there were many people coming and going, and they did not even have time to eat.) [32]They went away in the boat to a secluded place by themselves. (Mark 6:30–32)

After the disciples returned from their preaching ministry, Jesus sent them to a secluded place to rest. He knew both their physical and spiritual needs had to be met through time away from the activities of work and ministry. The experiences they received and the things they learned required time to settle. Only when they ceased their activity, rested their bodies and minds, and withdrew from those people and things that depleted their energy would they find nourishment for their souls.

Recently mixed concrete will never set as long as it stays in motion. However, as soon as the mixture is allowed to rest, it will settle and solidify. Similarly, we need time to be alone in silence, allowing the Spirit of God to settle the mishmash of life into something solid. He turns our churning chaos into settled clarity.

Compare Mark 1:35 and Matthew 14:23. Why do you think Jesus varied His time of solitude?

Solitude and ministry exist in tension with one another, yet they cannot be separated. Effective spiritual leaders must learn the discipline of keeping themselves in proper balance. Our purpose, like that of Christ, is to serve others, not to cloister ourselves away in order to hoard up spiritual treasures for our own enrichment. —*So, You Want to Be Like Christ?*

Leader Help

Jesus was not rigid in the timing of His solitude. Neither should we be. However, if we are not intentional about solitude, the danger of neglecting it is great. Schedule your time, but be flexible as special circumstances arise.

What are some benefits of having a scheduled, protected time set aside for silence and solitude?

What are some of the reasons why this time should be somewhat flexible?

Leader Help

Jesus would have had a lot of reasons to neglect this "down time"—for example, the demand of meeting the needs of the people, His desire to make the most of His time, or knowing that His time was short. Today we too have all sorts of "good" excuses for neglecting this time of rest and nourishment before God. But Jesus set the example of resting and encouraged the disciples to do the same, so we too must make silence and solitude a priority in our busy schedules.

Imagine you are one of the many men or women who followed Christ and His apostles around during His itinerant preaching. Give three good reasons that you might think Jesus's times of solitude away from ministering to people would be a waste of time.

What reasons do you have to neglect times of silence and solitude in your life and ministry?

Read Psalm 46. This psalm of confidence in God even in the midst of chaos is neatly divided into three sections by the pause *selah* (vv. 3, 7, 11). These three sections proclaim that God is our refuge in natural disasters (vv. 1–3); He is our stronghold in threatening warfare (vv. 4–7); and He is in control of our seemingly uncertain future (vv. 8–11).

If you've ever experienced the shock of a natural disaster, the fear of terrorism or warfare, or the anxiety of an uncertain future, how did you handle these distractions? Did God feel more present or more distant during these episodes in your life?

How does God's command to "cease" in Psalm 46:10 relate to God's promise of His presence with us in vv. 1, 5, 7, and 11?

How is trust in God essential to obedience of this command?

Give it some time. Your mind will flood with silly cares and useless observations. Usually the longer it's been and the busier you are, the longer it will take for your mind to calm down and grow quiet. Don't fight it. Don't rush it. And don't feel guilty. It's normal. Just let your mind run. Eventually, without trying and before you know it, your mind is still. Not empty; just quiet.—*So, You Want to Be Like Christ?*

Though many of us don't face daily terrors of natural disasters and war, we choose to keep constantly busy because of our anxiety about our future. We want control of our destinies, and making the time to stop and rest can seem like an added stress to our schedules.

Why does taking time to cease from activity in the midst of your own busy, demanding, chaotic schedule and circumstances require trust in God?

What exactly would you need to entrust to God in order to cease from activity?

STARTING YOUR JOURNEY . . .
We've discovered that just as the body needs *physical* rest and nourishment, so the spirit needs *spiritual* rest and nourishment that can only come from silence and solitude. Even Jesus and His disciples needed silence and solitude in the midst of ministry. However, the question most people ask is, "What do I do once I'm silent and alone?" The answer? *Listen*—not pray, not read Scripture, not even listen to inspiring preaching or music on the radio. In quietness, the Holy Spirit ministers to us by melding our experiences, the advice of godly counselors, and the wisdom of the Word of God. In a place of solitude, God's "small

sound of silence" (1 Kings 19:12) blows like a gentle breeze, driving the clutter from our minds.

From the time you saved through simplifying your schedule in the last lesson, set aside a specific time for silence and solitude this week. It might be in the morning, the evening, or anytime that works for you. Schedule your appointment with God and keep it.

Determine a place where you can be alone and uninterrupted. It might be in part of your home or away from home. Find a place that's secluded, yet not too remote that it becomes a burden just to get there. Write down a primary and a secondary option below.

As you begin your time of silence, simply kneel or sit silently before God. First, pray that He would clear the clutter from your mind, calm your soul, and refresh your spirit. Then do *nothing* for however long you've determined.

Leader Help

The practical application of silence and solitude is one of the most individualized disciplines. Some need very little time in silence and solitude. Some need hours a day. Some people find it easy to rest and to regain clarity; others prefer journaling to clarify their thoughts after a period of silence. Encourage group members to try different approaches and to share with each other things they tried and the results they experienced.

Select one of the following exercises for silence and solitude or create your own to put into practice over the next week or so.

❏ If you're having trouble clearing your mind of the worries and concerns of life during your time of silence, you might try using a "worry pad" to write down the things to which your mind keeps gravitating. Once you jot down your concerns, set the list aside. (We'll show you what to do with it in lesson 5.) This can help clear the reverberating worries from your mind and allow you to focus on listening to God in silence.

Leader Help

For additional suggestions on journaling, see the section entitled "Preserve What You Discover" in chapter 3 of *So, You Want to Be Like Christ*.

❏ After a time of silence, some find the practice of journaling to be helpful. There is no prescribed way to journal; most people simply write their thoughts down by hand in a personal notepad. This isn't the same as writing a diary or an organizer. It's usually not something you write daily. This is not a record of what you've done during the day or the week, but a record of your spiritual journey—what you discovered about God and your relationship with Him. Following times of silence and solitude with times of journaling may help you reflect on the clarity God reveals to you.

❏ Select one of the following verses to memorize. When you face the noise and bustle of a busy life, remember your verse and the value God places on silence and solitude.

_____ Psalm 62:1

_____ Lamentations 3:25–26

_____ Isaiah 30:15

In our crowded, noisy world, the discipline of seeking God in silence and solitude can minister peace and clarity to our cluttered minds and famished spirits. Taking time to focus completely on God, to surrender your time and activities to Him, to completely cease your activity for the sake of intimate, quiet communion is to offer yourself up for the nourishment only the Holy Spirit can provide. As you practice the discipline of silence and solitude between now and the next lesson, remind yourself that just as your physical body needs rest and nourishment, so does your soul. If Christ needed to retreat to a secluded place for rest, so do you.

Surrender:
Releasing Our Grip

Surrender:
Releasing Our Grip

THE HEART OF THE MATTER

Christ exemplified the most perfect act of surrender when He gave up His place in glory to come to earth, take on a human nature, and die for us. When we follow Christ's example and we surrender to God by faith those things that encumber our fulfillment of His purpose, we will be surprised by the freedom that comes! As we release our grip, we discover that the things we thought we needed to hold on to were in reality holding on to us. Along with this lesson, read chapter 4 of *So, You Want to Be Like Christ?*

Leader Help
By the end of this lesson, group members should be able to contrast Christlike surrender with an uncaring abandonment of important things in life. The members should also resolve to release their grip on and cease pursuing whatever keeps them from completely trusting God.

YOU ARE HERE . . .

The Academy Award-winning film *Terms of Endearment* opens with a scene any parent can relate to. The main character, Aurora, enters a dark and quiet nursery to check on her infant daughter. She leans into the crib and doesn't hear the child breathing. Wondering whether the baby is still alive, she resorts to pinching her until she wakes up. As the movie depicts, during the next several decades Aurora's original care and concern for her daughter grow into an overbear-

Leader Help
Discuss the results of last week's activity, having people share their personal experiences with silence and solitude. Encourage members to persevere through any frustrations or disappointments.

ing attitude of control that affects her daughter's marriage and children. Aurora's problem? She couldn't let go.

For you it might not be a son or daughter. It may be your plans, a position, a relationship, or a material object. We all hold on to something, either afraid to let go or perhaps unwilling to entrust it to somebody else. Maybe we're afraid of losing it. Maybe we believe that letting something go means we must no longer care for or about it. Maybe holding something close is the way we show our love or a way we can feel secure. Humans naturally find it very difficult to release our grip and surrender control.

 List the different types of insurance you have. What is each designed to protect or replace?

Leader Help
Encourage creative, abstract thinking in these categories, such as memories, senses, and sense of humor.

 From the following four categories, what other things—either material or immaterial—would you insure if insurance was available and affordable?

Possessions:

Positions:

Plans:

People:

How would you respond if you lost these things today?

Read Hebrews 12:1–3. In verse 1, what does the author tell his readers to set aside?

I am convinced of this: the author of Hebrews cannot conceive our successfully running life's race without first deciding to trust God— *really* relying on Him. And that kind of trust begins by surrendering to Him.—*So, You Want to Be Like Christ?*

According to verses 2–3, what should be our focus in the Christian life?

What things in your life are bogging you down as you run toward this goal? What encumbrances do you need to release that are making you weary or causing you to lose heart?

Leader Help

Some people may fear that loosening our grip on important things means we don't care about them anymore. In many cases letting go and turning things over to God's control demonstrates an even greater care or concern. Perhaps somebody can share a specific example of this from his or her own experience.

Can you care about something dearly and still let it go? How would you differentiate between releasing control of something versus becoming indifferent?

 DISCOVERING THE WAY . . .

All to Jesus I surrender,
All to Him I freely give;
I will ever love and trust Him,
In His presence daily live.

I surrender all,
I surrender all.
All to Thee, my blessed Savior,
I surrender all.[1]

How many of us can sing those words and honestly mean that we've surrendered everything to Christ? Even if we say it, how many of us really understand what that means? Let's be honest. Many of us feel more like Ananias and Sapphira, who kept a little back from the sale of their land, than like Barnabas, who cast everything from his sale at the feet of the apostles (compare Acts 4:34–37 to Acts 5:1–11). Unlike Christ, our human tendency is to *avoid* surrendering anything.

[5]Have this attitude in yourselves which was also in Christ Jesus, [6]who, although He existed in the form of

God, did not regard equality with God a thing to be grasped, [7]but emptied Himself, taking the form of a bond-servant, and being made in the likeness of men. [8]Being found in appearance as a man, He humbled Himself, by becoming obedient to the point of death, even death on a cross. (Philippians 2:5–8)

 According to Philippians 2:6, what did the Son of God surrender?

 In verse 7, what was the result of this surrender?

Leader Help

It's important to emphasize that Christ did not give up any of His deity or His divine attributes (see "Study Christ" section of chapter 4 of *So, You Want to Be Like Christ?*). As you discuss this issue, be reminded that Jesus remained completely God but took on a full human nature. In this "emptying," Christ surrendered possessions, position, and plans, but He did not lose any of His deity.

 When the eternal Son of God took on humanity, what did He surrender in each of the following areas?

Possessions (see 2 Corinthians 8:9).

Position (see John 17:5).

Plans (see Luke 22:42).

DIGGING DEEPER

 Christ's Extreme Surrender
Philippians 2:6 says Christ did not regard equality with God a "thing to be grasped."

This phrase has been understood in a variety of ways. Does it mean "something to hold on to" or "something to be snatched away"?[2]

Those who interpret it as "something to hold on to" understand it to mean the Son existed in an equal position with the Father (see John 1:1) but voluntarily surrendered His position in submission to the Father by taking on humanity and becoming man (see John 1:14). On the other hand, if it means "something to be snatched away," the emphasis is on the eternal order of the Trinity: the Son acts in submission to the Father's will though they exist eternally as equally divine—the same in power but distinct in activities. The Son of God, while equal to the Father, willingly surrendered His heavenly position and submitted to His Father's will.

Either interpretation presents us with a stunning description of Christ's surrender of His high position in order to accomplish God's will and save humanity from their sins. No illustration of human surrender matches this supreme example of Christ.

Thankfully, hymns like "I Surrender All" can express the attitude of our hearts, the ideal toward which we strive, even if we're not quite there yet. We desire to be able to surrender, to take that step of heroic faith and turn over to God everything—our worries, our fears, our idols, even the blessings of God that bring us such joy. Yet, in reality, the majority of us, even on our most spiritual days, share the sentiments of the father of the demonized boy in Mark 9:24: "I do believe; help my unbelief."

Surrender is excruciating. It's easy to develop attachments that hinder us in our growth toward Christlikeness. However, as we study Christ and measure ourselves against His example, we'll learn to hold on to people and things more loosely, to release our selfish grip on whatever holds us back and turn over important things to God, whose grip can never grow weary. Hebrews 12:1–2 reminds us to lay aside every encumbrance as well as sin, to run the race set before us, and to keep our eyes on Jesus. We want to do just that.

 In Philippians 2:5, Paul tells us to have the same attitude Christ had when He surrendered His possessions, position, and plans in submission to the Father's will. What specific possessions, position, plans, or even people are you holding on to a bit too tightly?

Possessions:

Position:

Plans:

People:

Keep Jesus as your standard. All other human examples are driven by a survival instinct, an internal compulsion to preserve and nurture self. Only Christ modeled godly selflessness throughout His entire life. While others seek to preserve their own lives, He came to lay His down. —*So, You Want to Be Like Christ?*

How has trying to maintain control over these things distracted you from intimate fellowship with Christ?

You've considered what Christ *surrendered* in leaving His place of heavenly glory. Now examine what Christ *gained* in giving these up. Read Philippians 2:9–11. What does this passage say Christ gained after the ultimate surrender of His very life?

Leader Help

This question is somewhat subjective. You may need to prepare in advance a response from your own reflection. What types of benefits have you experienced by giving up material possessions, passing up a promotion, releasing a loved one to God's care, or another example?

Have you ever given up or surrendered something and gained something better? What were the benefits of surrendering? Share your experience with the group or write about it below.

In the following passages, what attitudes or things were holding people back from having a more intimate relationship with Christ?

Mark 10:17–22

Mark 10:35–45

1 Peter 5:5–7

Surrender is tough at the start, especially if you are a selfish kind of person, a little spoiled, a little pampered, a little overly indulged. Your old self will whine and fight for survival! Surrendering is not for the pampered. God honors those who pay the price to be like Him: selfless. That's why surrendering plays such a dominant role in putting self in its place. —*So, You Want to Be Like Christ?*

STARTING YOUR JOURNEY...
Christ surrendered all. He released His grip on His heavenly position of glory and authority. He let go of the riches of glory in exchange for the rags of a manger. He submitted to the plans of the Father even to the point of an agonizing death. He exchanged intimate heavenly fellowship with the Father and Spirit for the companionship of men and women who constantly misunderstood Him. Why did He do it? To restore humanity to intimate fellowship with God through unity with Him.

Christ had no self-interest. Each step downward was part of His total attitude of complete surrender. Was it easy? Not at all. Was it painless? Hardly. But was it worth it? Absolutely. And it's also worth it for us in our own lives as we follow Christ's example.

In this lesson you've identified various ways that possessions, positions, plans, and people may be encumbering your walk due to your selfish pursuit or your white-knuckled grip. It's time to surrender these things to God. This may mean physically and literally giving them away, or it may mean symbolically and mentally handing these over to God's care and protection by faith. Place a check mark next to the area below in which you most need to surrender, and write down the specific person or thing on which you will release your grip.

_____ Possessions:

_____ Position:

_____ Plans:

_____ People:

Now select from among the following activities the one that is most appropriate to your unique situation, and write a commitment to complete it over the next few days:

Leader Help

Each group member should be encouraged to select an activity or to modify one of the following sets of activities to work on over the next few days. You may want to ask specific people to be prepared to share their experience in exercising surrender. Close in prayer, asking God to assist your group in fulfilling their commitments to surrender all to God by faith.

❏ **Release Your Possessions.** On a separate sheet of paper, make a list of material possessions you're holding close, then bring each item before the Lord in prayer.

Release each one by name to God. Declare that He is the owner of each item, not you. If you're married, do this activity with your spouse.

OR

Consider giving away something of value that you may even be treating as an idol. (An idol could be anything that you allow to occupy a higher place than God in your life.) Think of things you spend a lot of time maintaining or managing.

❏ **Release Your Position.** List below all the titles, degrees, roles, or awards/achievements you have received.

Read Philippians 3:8. How does this passage improve or correct your perspective on your accomplishments and position?

OR

Is there a position you are desperately striving to attain? Release your grip on that ambition, and surrender your control of the situation and outcome to God's goodness and sovereignty. You may want to read 1 Chronicles 29:12 for some perspective.

❏ **Release Your Plans.** List below future plans and goals you hope to achieve in the next five to ten years.

Read James 4:13–16 and Proverbs 27:1. Take time to pray, releasing these to God. Surrender your entire future to Him, asking Him to conform your life and goals to His purposes.

OR

If you've been trying to secure a particular plan or set a specific course for your future but have been increasingly frustrated because it hasn't been realized, consider that you may need to release it into God's care. Perhaps God has greater plans in store for you. Or perhaps He will work out your plans in His way after you've released your own control of the situation. You can consciously change your attitude toward this now in prayer.

I urge you. Release your grip. Surrender it all to God, including your anxiety. If you still have your emotions wrapped around some issue involving a possession, a job or role, a particular expectation for the future, or a relationship, you aren't fully relying on God. As long as you fail to surrender to Him, you're holding on to anxiety. Stop. Let go. You're delaying the surprise God has waiting for you.—*So, You Want to Be Like Christ?*

❏ **Release Your People.** Sometimes we hold on tightly to our loved ones out of care and concern. However, often the most caring thing we can do is release them to the care of God. His plans for people are not ours. Whom are you holding on to with a tight grip, either because you are afraid to lose them or desperate to gain them?

Take some time now to pray and turn over to God's care and protection this person and your relationship with him or her. Now, take any steps you believe are wise and necessary to demonstrate this release. That may mean granting that person freedom—even freedom to make mistakes. It may mean relating to him or her in a different way. Describe below your course of action; then do it.

OR

For one full day, try to focus on serving others above yourself. Think of specific people, specific needs, and specific ways in which you can surrender your own possessions, position, and plans for the sake of others. After you have done this, describe below the benefits or frustrations you experienced.

As you look to Christ and seek to model His ultimate example of voluntary surrender and dependence on God, decide to do as He did. Surrender your possessions. Surrender your power. Surrender your plans. Surrender the people you love. Surrender all to the Father's care and control, and trust Him to manage them better than you can. If the eternal Son of God did it, He can empower you to do it too.

Surrender is not always a one-time decision. It may be something you do daily or even moment by moment. It's not easy to give up things to which you've grown attached, but there will be benefits. Surrender will result in surprises you would never otherwise experience. In fact, the greater the struggle to surrender, the greater the surprise God has in store for you. As long as you fail to surrender all to Him, you're holding on to anxiety. Stop, release your grip, and accept the surprise awaiting you.

Leader Help

If appropriate in your group, consider singing the hymn "I Surrender All" or another hymn or chorus that reflects personal devotion and surrender of everything to God.

Prayer:
Calling Out

Prayer:
Calling Out

THE HEART OF THE MATTER

Prayer is the God-ordained alternative to worry. As we lift our joys and burdens to God through intimate communication with Him, we become more like Christ. Entrusting every predicament and every dilemma to our heavenly Father, we learn to live in total dependence on Him. Along with this lesson, read chapter 5 of *So, You Want to Be Like Christ?*

YOU ARE HERE ...

The pressures of our times have caught many of us in the web of one of the most menacing sins in the Christian life: worry. Worry is not an emotion; it's a choice. Worry is choosing to fret and strategize instead of entrusting an issue to God's care. Worry is wrestling with the bully of anxiety on your own rather than letting the Father fight your battles for you. The choice to worry creates unrest, prolongs uneasiness and, if left unchallenged, churns our waves of anxiety into a storm of emotions.

Leader Help

By the end of this lesson, group members should understand that the proper response to worry is prayer. They'll be motivated not only to pray rather than worry, but also to take steps to establish prayer as a regular discipline in their lives.

Leader Help

Take a few minutes to discuss group members' practice of surrendering since the last meeting. Discuss how prayer may have had a part in their exercise of the discipline of surrender.

If you could eliminate one major issue that causes you persistent emotional concern, what would it be?

 What circumstance keeps this issue on your mind?

 How has your choice to worry improved the situation?

 How has it made it worse?

What are the causes of worry, anxiety, or concern in the following passages?

Psalm 38:18

1 Corinthians 7:32–35

2 Corinthians 11:28

Philippians 2:20

What does the variety of these causes tell you about deep, emotional concern? Is it avoidable? Is it necessarily wrong? When does genuine concern for something or someone turn into worry?

In the following passages, what results come from worry if it isn't handled properly?

Proverbs 12:25

Matthew 13:22

Leader Help

We should never attempt to avoid having serious, emotional concern for people and circumstances. Concern is usually legitimate, and compassion is never a sin. The problem lies not in experiencing emotional turmoil but in the ways we respond to it. Describe a healthy example of concern that causes you to respond to something appropriately in prayer and godly action, then illustrate how a response to this same concern can cross the line into worry and anxiety.

Put succinctly, prayer is communicating with God. A conversation that can be spoken or silent, and even expressed in song. Many of the psalms are prayers set to music. A primary purpose of prayer is connecting with God in order to transfer His will into your life. —*So, You Want to Be Like Christ?*

What personal experiences have you had with these consequences of worrying?

Read Matthew 6:25–34. About what things does Jesus say we should not be anxious?

About which of these things do you sometimes experience anxiety?

What reasons does Christ give for not worrying about these things?

DISCOVERING THE WAY . . .

Prayer is talking with God. It's more than just two strangers chatting about the weather, two chums cutting up over old times, or two business associates discussing the details of the next official transaction. Prayer is a conversation between you and the sovereign God of the universe fueled by a longing to know Him intimately and experientially, to know what He desires, and to receive the blessings of a relationship with God.

Prayer is not bargaining or pleading or attempting to extract from God an outcome we desire. No amount of pleading will convince Him to be more merciful and kind than He already is. He will always act in our best interest, even if we never utter a word to Him (Romans 8:28). Yet we are invited to bring our burdens to Him, to lay our concerns upon Him, and to experience a blissful alternative to a life of worry.

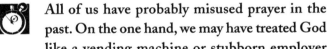

All of us have probably misused prayer in the past. On the one hand, we may have treated God like a vending machine or stubborn employer rather than a loving heavenly Father who responds to us in ways that glorify Him and demonstrate His love for us. On the other hand, we may have chosen to handle things on our own and neglected prayer altogether . . . or gone to the other extreme, replacing our own timely action with a prayer that shirked responsibility. Share an experience from your life in which you abused prayer.

Leader Help

In preparation for this question, review the four perils in chapter 5 of *So, You Want to Be Like Christ?* There you'll find detailed descriptions of these various perils of prayer that may help you in discussion. Not all group members will feel comfortable sharing, but encourage a couple who are willing to illustrate how a misunderstanding of prayer can cause frustration.

Leader Help

This first series of questions explores common misunderstandings and misuses of prayer. The information here could be used in conjunction with that question for further clarification or a more in-depth treatment. If group members did their work in advance, their answers to the following questions will help in the discussion.

There are a lot of perilous misconceptions about prayer. Of the following perils, over which have you stumbled?

Irresponsibility. Prayer is not meant to *replace* human action or responsibility. The two work together in a way that is unexplainable. How have you used prayer to neglect responsibility?

Misperception. If you picture God as an angry ogre, your prayers will be timid and few. If you picture Him as a pampering parent, they will be self-centered and greedy. A proper perception of God as the loving, just, all-powerful heavenly Father will put your prayer life into perspective. How has your perception of God sometimes (mis)shaped your prayers?

Overcommitment. If you're too busy to pray, you'll miss out on the benefits that come from the investment of prayer. How have you sometimes allowed activities to drown out your prayer life? It might be necessary for you to revisit the chapter on the discipline of simplicity in order to free up time for prayer.

Oversimplification. While our prayers should be simple, sometimes we oversimplify prayer into an equation to get what we want, treating God as an impersonal vending machine or a scientific mechanism that works perfectly, if we just do it correctly. That's more like magic than prayer. How have you treated prayer like a formula rather than an intimate conversation with a real, living being?

According to 1 John 5:14–15, does God give us everything we request? What do you feel are the limits?

In 2 Corinthians 12:7–10, how did God provide for Paul in spite of the fact that He didn't answer his prayer in the way he asked?

God isn't a vending machine. Yet, too often we come to Him hungry and ready to trade our sacrifices for whatever will fill our need. Popular televangelist figures would have us believe that we're still hungry because we didn't pray correctly. . . . They would have us think that without the right formula, God will not act on our behalf—that He withholds His goodness until we approach Him using the right ritual. —*So, You Want to Be Like Christ?*

GRAY MATTERS
Will God Answer a Lousy Prayer?

As simple as prayer is, a large degree of mystery is also involved. Though there are right and wrong ways to pray, prayer itself is a personal, subjective experience of God. There are rarely clear principles about how or why God responds in the ways He does.

We know that in His sovereign plan, God works out all things for our good (Romans 8:28) and that He always responds to our prayers (1 John 5:14–15). Scripture presents a great variety of prayers that were answered—often in ways that surprise us. God answered Paul's prayer for freedom from his "thorn in the flesh" with a no (2 Corinthians 12:7–10). He answered the petition of the Israelites for a king "like the other nations" according to their will, even though the answer involved negative consequences (1 Samuel 8:19–22). In the case of Solomon, God answered his prayer for wisdom, then added blessings for which he didn't ask (2 Chronicles 1:11–12). In short, in concert with our prayers, God works in various ways to bring about His perfect will, as well as our ultimate good.

Take time to discuss some of the following mysteries of prayer, remembering these two principles: God's sovereign will and His perfect goodness.

Do you believe God would ever give you something you pray for even though it may not be good for you? How does your answer reflect God's sovereignty and goodness? What scriptures address this question?

What does "good" mean in Romans 8:28 and James 1:17? Is "good" in our minds the same as "good" in God's plan? Be sure to consider both long-term and short-term perspectives. Explain your answer.

Are blessings from God dependent on prayer? If you completely ceased praying, would God stop working in your life? Support your answer with Scripture and/or your life experiences.

Use a Bible concordance, credible theological book on prayer, or other tools to help inform your answers. Also, consider how your experience with answered and unanswered prayer may contribute to your understanding of these issues.

God wants good things for every son and daughter, and He wants to bless us, but never at the expense of our holiness. He may choose to deny our request for one blessing if the refusal paves the way for a greater one. —*So, You Want to Be Like Christ?*

In the previous lesson we focused on specific areas in our lives we needed to surrender to God. One of the repeated means of surrender was prayer—making a conscious decision to relinquish our control and turn over to God whatever encumbers us. When we hold on to people or things with a tight grip, the results are worry, fear, and anxiety. How are all these problems released? Through prayer.

> [6]Be anxious for nothing, but in everything by prayer and supplication with thanksgiving let your requests be made known to God. [7]And the peace of God, which surpasses all comprehension, will guard your hearts and your minds in Christ Jesus. (Philippians 4:6–7)

This passage may be very familiar to some, but sometimes seeing it differently can be very revealing. The following exercise will help you look at the details of this powerful passage on prayer in a fresh light.

 In Philippians 4:6, circle the words *but, in, by, and,* and *with.*

 Underline the two commands in Philippians 4:6. (Hint: there is one command before the circled words and one after.)

 Fill in the following chart that reorganizes Philippians 4:6 according to the main commands and the *means (or methods)* Paul proposes for fulfilling the commands:

1. Be _____ _____ _____ – but . . . let _____ _____ _____ _____ _____ _____ ____.

2. in _____

3. by _____ and _____

4. with _____

According to line 1 of the diagram, what are your two alternative responses to persistent concern over something?

 According to line 2, what things should you make known to God in order to be free from anxiety?

 In line 3, what are the means (or methods) by which you make your requests known to God?

 In line 4, what is the manner or attitude in which you ought to approach God?

Before this day is done, you will have another occasion to choose between worry and prayer. Determine now what you will do. Decide now that when the crisis arises you will transform the worry into prayer. If at the end of praying, your emotions are still in turmoil, pray more. By cultivating the discipline of prayer, you will discover the ability to remain calm and quiet. —*So, You Want to Be Like Christ?*

In Philippians 4:7, what is the promise to those who choose prayer instead of worry?

 Recall the one area of anxiety you wanted to eliminate at the beginning of this lesson (page 74). How can your choice to worry attack your heart (emotions) and mind (thoughts) if you persist?

Leader Help

For the study questions on pages 84–86, the group may want to focus on the concluding questions and overall teaching of the passages rather than examining each scripture in detail.

In the following passages, how is prayer made a top priority? Jot down the key words that indicate the importance of prayer.

1 Timothy 2:1

Acts 2:42

Acts 6:2–4

1 Thessalonians 5:17

To what evidence in your own life can you point to demonstrate that prayer is a top priority for you?

Besides a cure for worry, there are many other benefits and effects of prayer. From the following passages, summarize in a few words the effects of prayer:

James 1:5

James 5:14–16

Ephesians 1:18

Philippians 1:9

2 Thessalonians 3:1

What an astounding gift God has given us in prayer! Which of these benefits is most encouraging to you based on your unique situation today?

Having a deep, persistent concern for a problem is not the same as worry. Worry is choosing to fret and churn instead of turning it completely over to God. Worry is wrestling with anxiety on your own rather than releasing it to the Father. —*So, You Want to Be Like Christ?*

Start your day with prayer and continue praying off and on through the day. Pray as you drive. Pray at work. Pray before your lunch break. Pray when you get that difficult phone call. Pray when you are disappointed by something. Pray when surprises come. Pray when you triumph. Pray in the midst of painful news. Pray without ceasing . . . *literally. —So, You Want to Be Like Christ?*

In the following passages, for which categories of people should we pray?

Matthew 5:44

1 Thessalonians 5:25

1 Timothy 2:1–2

Go back and jot down the names of people you know in each of these categories.

STARTING YOUR JOURNEY . . .

The peace that comes from God and the protection of our hearts and minds through prayer will bring us joy even in the midst of troubling circumstances. Yet our primary goal in calling out to God through a life of prayer is not to make our daily existence easier or more enjoyable. The goal can be summed up in four words: intimacy with the Almighty.

However, if we're going to have an intimate relationship with God, we need to do more than just read, study, and talk about prayer. We need to pray.

Return to the area of continuing concern you desire to eliminate. You may not be able to immediately rid yourself of it. Whether the matter is harmless or potentially carries grave consequences, your choice to worry about it causes problems. You can take your anxiety about it to God, who is ready to receive you with open arms. Use the following prayer as a launching point; fill in the space with whatever troubles you today—that one matter that plagues your heart and mind. If there are elements of this prayer that don't fit your particular situation, change it appropriately. Remember that surrender is a very large component of prayer. You are allowing God to have His way, not convincing Him that your way is right.

Kind and gracious Father,

I confess that I am deeply concerned about
_____. I've worried and fretted about this, and it repeatedly returns to my mind. I've tried to find a solution, but the matter persists. Sometimes I cannot understand why You, who have the power to do all things, have not acted. I don't understand why You allow bad circumstances to continue unresolved. But I also realize that I know almost nothing compared to what You know.

I accept that this matter is beyond my ability to resolve. Everything I've tried has come to nothing and possibly made things worse. Please give me the grace to accept this truth and to accept that You may not choose to intervene in the way I desire. Please comfort me as I accept whatever You choose to do, whenever You choose to do it, even if Your actions confuse or frustrate me.

Father, I release _____ into Your hands, into Your care, for You to do with

God is never too busy, never sleeps, never has His mind so occupied with running the universe that He will not hear you. And yet, never forget that an answer to prayer doesn't mean that He will solve our problems the way *we* want them solved. But He will hear our requests and respond with solutions— sometimes surprising ones— that not only address our concerns but deepen our faith in His wisdom and strengthen our confidence in His sovereignty. —*So, You Want to Be Like Christ?*

as You please. Help me to act only when You create an opportunity and only after I have measured my actions against Scripture and the wise counsel of a mature fellow believer. And I trust that this experience will ultimately prove to be for my good as You have promised. *Though I don't understand, I thank You for the good You are about to do.*

I praise You and thank You for what You will do, in the name of Your Son, Jesus Christ. Amen.

To apply the principles we've studied, select at least one of the following application activities or design your own to implement this week. Be prepared to share the results with your group at the beginning of your next meeting.

❏ If, as you worked through this lesson, you were able to isolate things and people you should pray for, record them on a prayer list and pray through this list each day in the coming week.

❏ If your watch, computer, or other electronic device has the capability, set it to alert you each hour to remind you to pray throughout the day about specific requests.

❏ In the lesson on silence and solitude, we suggested keeping a "worry pad" to write down the things that distracted you in moments of silence. If you did that, take the things from your "worry pad" and put them on your prayer list. Turn these over to God through a prayer similar to the one suggested above.

❏ Make a commitment that each time you feel inner turmoil, physical effects of anxiety, or stress, you will take that as a prompter to pray.

❏ Ask your spouse, children, or close friends what things are worrying them or making them anxious, then pray for them both in person and in your private prayer time.

❏ Establish a consistent family prayer time. Keep a family prayer log or prayer journal that indicates when specific requests were prayed for and how God answered those prayers.

❏ Share your prayer requests with others and comfort others by letting them know when you pray for them.

❏ Ask other believers what things they do in the discipline of prayer that prove to be effective for them. There's not just one way to pray, so you may find other creative ways to exercise this discipline.

The God-ordained alternative to choosing worry is to lift your concerns to God in prayer, which is a deep, personal communication with the living God that brings your burdens and requests to Him in faith. When you pray, you'll find yourself moving closer to the goal of becoming more like Christ. You'll enjoy an intimate relationship with God through a life of complete dependence upon Him for everything and a constant attitude of thanksgiving for what He has done, is doing, and will do in your life.

Praying with frequency gives us the readiness to pray again as needed from moment to moment. The more we pray, the more we think to pray, and as we see the results of prayer—the responses of our Father to our requests—our confidence in God's power spills over into other areas of our life.[1] —Dallas Willard

Leader Help
When you close this session, you may want to break into pairs and have each person pray for the other's requests. Or assign each person or couple another person or couple to pray for during the week. Ask that people be ready to share what they experienced in the next study time.

Humility:
Bowing Low

Humility:
Bowing Low

THE HEART OF THE MATTER

True humility stems from a realistic understanding of one's gifts, training, and skills and a contentment with one's God-designed purpose in life, whether lowly or exalted. Following the example of Christ, we express this attitude of humility through selfless attitudes and actions that seek the well-being of others. Along with this lesson, read chapter 6 of *So, You Want to Be Like Christ?*

YOU ARE HERE . . .

According to Jesus, the path to greatness in the kingdom of God winds through the valley of selflessness. He led the way by becoming the servant of all, the quintessential example of humility, and He invites us to follow. Yet this path is not an easy one. Few people today choose its uncertain, winding course.

Leader Help

By the end of this lesson, group members should recognize that humility is an action and that exaltation is God's prerogative, not ours. They should also seek contentment in whatever position God has for them and take steps to actively put others before themselves.

Leader Help

Take a few minutes at the start of this lesson to explore group members' practice of prayer since the last meeting. Discuss how they specifically applied the exercises at the end of the previous lesson and any altered perspectives they might have experienced.

Leader Help
In group discussion, several members may share their answers and briefly explain why they selected a particular person.

 Who do you think the world would view as the greatest living person? Why?

 Besides Jesus Christ, who do you think Christians would view as the greatest living person? Why?

 How did Jesus describe His own path to greatness in Mark 9:31?

 Read Mark 9:33–35. How did Jesus's words in verse 35 oppose the disciples' perceived path to greatness?

 Do the people you identified as "greatest" in the eyes of the world and the church measure up to Christ's idea of greatness? Why or why not?

Consider the unique gifts, abilities, training, and skills you have discovered or developed in your life. List at least three below. What would you consider to be your passion?

Your passion:

Next, what position in either ministry or career do you feel would best fit your qualifications?

If you're not currently working in that field or position, are you preparing for that position? How?

What positions or activities that you've done in the past do you now consider to be beneath your present skill sets, gifts, and training?

As you examine your own life, expectations, plans, and pursuits, are you on the world's path to exaltation or on Christ's path?

Describe a person you believe to be a model of humility. What is it about that person's attitude that makes you regard him or her as humble?

Leader Help

People generally fall into one of two camps: either they will find it easy to list their natural abilities and gifts, or they will find it difficult. Some group members may feel they have nothing to offer or that the skills they have do not qualify as tools for service. We are made in God's image, and we have been given His Spirit. Everyone has something to offer. If a group member has trouble coming up with a list, ask other members to share positive traits they have noticed in that person and what positions might fit them.

Genuinely humble people who have a desire to seek the well-being of others are generally very secure people. They are fully aware of their gifts, their training, their experience, and all the attributes that make them successful at whatever they do. That security—that honest, healthy self-assessment—results in more than a humble constitution; it translates into actions that can be observed, actions that we will want to emulate.
—*So, You Want to Be Like Christ?*

What specific actions has this person displayed that demonstrate this attitude?

How is this person viewed by other believers or by unbelievers? Do they admire this person's humility or regard it as a weakness?

 DISCOVERING THE WAY . . .

Let's face it. Humility is something we like to see in others but have difficulty putting into practice in our own lives. In our ego-driven, me-centered world, there are a lot of misconceptions about humility. Some think humility stems from a poor self-image or reflects weakness in a lack of confidence. Others treat it like a personality trait some people are born with or a spiritual gift that marks a select number of saints. However, humility is a Christlike quality that can be nurtured in all believers.

[36]And He said to them, "What do you want Me to do for you?" [37]They said to Him, "Grant that we may sit, one on Your right and one on Your left, in Your glory." [38]But Jesus said to them, "You do not know what you are asking. Are you able to drink the cup that I drink, or to be baptized with the baptism with which I am baptized?" [39]They said to Him,

"We are able." And Jesus said to them, "The cup that I drink you shall drink; and you shall be baptized with the baptism with which I am baptized. [40]But to sit on My right or on My left, this is not Mine to give; but it is for those for whom it has been prepared." [41]Hearing this, the ten began to feel indignant with James and John. [42]Calling them to Himself, Jesus said to them, "You know that those who are recognized as rulers of the Gentiles lord it over them; and their great men exercise authority over them. [43]But it is not this way among you, but whoever wishes to become great among you shall be your servant; [44]and whoever wishes to be first among you shall be slave of all. [45]For even the Son of Man did not come to be served, but to serve, and to give His life a ransom for many." (Mark 10:36–45)

 When Jesus asked James and John, "What do you want Me to do for you," for what did they ask (Mark 10:36–37)?

 In what way could this request have been motivated by a desire to serve others?

Read Mark 9:31–32, then examine Jesus's figurative language in Mark 10:38–39. What was Jesus referring to when he talked about His "drink" and "baptism"?

 According to Mark 10:40 and Matthew 20:23, who is responsible for positions in the kingdom?

Contrast Jesus's greatness in the world's eyes with greatness in the kingdom of God, according to Jesus's description.

Worldly Greatness (Mark 10:42)	Kingdom Greatness (Mark 10:43–44)

For what two reasons did Jesus say He came (Mark 10:45)?

"to _____" and

"to _____"

When it comes to our own paths in ministry or career, we usually plan for a steady climb up the ladder of success or a periodic advancement to a better position with each step we take. Rarely do we anticipate a step downward in pay, responsibility, or recognition. When that happens, we may feel like failures or believe we're victims of injustice.

 Recalling Christ's path of humility and exaltation, from Philippians 2:6–11 briefly describe Christ's present position at the Father's right hand.

 Which of the following diagrams best represents Christ's path to exaltation?

A   B   C

Which diagram most represents your desired career or ministry path?

A   B   C

What is it that prompts humility within me? What do I need to think or to do that will allow me to think less of myself and more of others? A full appreciation for the sacrifice that Christ made for me will do that. Everything I have, everything I am, every good thing I enjoy would not be possible were it not for Him. The more I understand the price He paid, the less room I have for pride. — *So, You Want to Be Like Christ?*

 In Philippians 2:3–4, how does Paul ask us to apply the principle of Christ's ultimate example of humility that he described in verses 5–11?

Mark 10:40–45 teaches that our own worldly view of greatness and the world's path to exaltation are completely opposed to Christ's. For Jesus, greatness came through humility, putting others above Himself, serving, and giving everything He had. Our own responsibility is to keep our eyes on Christ's example and to live humble lives for others by selfless acts of service. This takes confidence in our God and contentment with our circumstances, trusting that God will exalt us when and how He chooses, according to His goodness and sovereignty. Exaltation itself is not our responsibility, but God's prerogative.

According to the following passages, who is responsible for promotion, and who is exalted?

Daniel 4:17

James 4:10

1 Peter 5:5–6

If you were to present your career or ministry plan to Jesus Christ, face to face, what specific attitudes and actions do you think He would point out? Why?

In the following passages, how are the humble blessed?

Psalm 10:17

Psalm 25:9

Psalm 37:11

Proverbs 11:2

Proverbs 29:23

Isaiah 66:2

Leader Help
If you choose to study these passages in the small-group meeting, select three or four that you feel best illustrate the principle and focus on them.

Read Jesus's example of humility in John 13:3–5. Though He was aware of and confident in His relationship with the Father, the reality of His person, and His role in the Father's plan, Jesus took on the actions of a servant when He washed the disciples' feet.

Put no trust in your own learning nor in the cunning of any man, but rather in the grace of God Who helps the humble and humbles the proud.[1] —Thomas à Kempis

What does this example of Jesus teach us about the act of humility as it relates to our gifts, abilities, training, or skills?

How does Peter's reaction in John 13:6–8 illustrate our worldly resistance to acts of humility?

According to Ephesians 1:3–14, what is the reality of your own spiritual identity and position in Christ? Select and list below three truths from that passage that stand out most for you.

How does a firm confidence in our own identity in Christ free us to display humility toward others?

A key to humility is contentment with what we have and with the position in which God has placed us. Read the following passages and summarize in your own words how each passage relates to contentment with humility. What roles do external circumstances play in each?

2 Corinthians 12:7–10

Philippians 4:11–13

1 Timothy 6:6–10

Humility—the discipline of putting others ahead of self, the choice to value others above self—is, at its core, a matter of faith. —*So, You Want to Be Like Christ?*

 STARTING YOUR JOURNEY . . .
Humility is the choice to put the interests of others ahead of our own. It's a decision motivated by gratitude and powered by faith. Christ humbled Himself and died a criminal's death to spare us the damnation we deserve. If gratitude dwells in our hearts, humility will be a frequent house-guest. Furthermore, the discipline of putting others ahead of ourselves requires faith. If we genuinely believe that God cares for us and desires our best, and if we have confidence that our spiritual identity in Christ is unchangeable, then we don't need to be consumed with serving our own interests. We can afford to focus attention on meeting the needs of others because we have every confidence that God will spare nothing of His infinite resources to turn our poverty into His abundance.

We have seen that humility, though an attitude of the heart, is an *action* first and foremost. Christ's own humility is not simply asserted, but it's demonstrated in the most extreme act imaginable—becoming human and dying for the sins of the world. Do you want to be like Christ? Nurture the discipline of humility by actively choosing to place the needs and welfare of others above your own. In light of Christ's example of humility, let's refocus our attention from ourselves to others.

Leader Help

Because of the unique nature of this discipline, it might be inappropriate to share "accomplishments" in humility in a group setting. Instead, encourage group members to take this task seriously and keep each other in prayer as they select their exercises and attempt to nurture a humble attitude with actions.

Select one of the following options for exercising the discipline of humility, or come up with your own to put into practice this week. Write the action you choose in the following space; then do it.

This week, by God's grace, I will . . .

❏ In light of your unique gifts, abilities, and training, in what ways could you serve others? As you answer this question, begin by considering the needs of others first rather than the tasks or positions that would satisfy your own need or desire for participation. Whom in particular could you help and in what specific ways could you serve them?

❏ Think of a specific task for which your church is desperate for volunteers. It may be helping with children's ministry, outreach, or "mundane" tasks such as cleaning the church. You may want to look in your church bulletin or call your pastor to find out what job nobody seems to want. Temporarily set aside your unique gifts, abilities, talents, and skills and give your time and energy to help meet this need.

❏ In your home, what household chore is neglected because nobody wants to do it? Claim that chore as your own and do it quietly, *without complaining or expecting any recognition!*

❏ If you know of a need that you could meet in the life of an individual or family, do so anonymously.

❏ Be generous with your compliments of others and spare talking about yourself. To consistently remind yourself to do this, write it in your prayer list and pray about demonstrating humility in your words each day, then evaluate how you did the previous day. Think of specific people you can compliment, and don't let an opportunity pass you by.

We can only pursue humility as an action, a behavior, not as a quality of character. And yet, if we exercise the discipline long enough, it will inevitably dominate our nature without our knowing what happened. — *So, You Want to Be Like Christ?*

❏ Think of some other specific act of humility you could do that would place the interests and needs of others above your own or reverse the trend of selfish ambition and aggressive pursuit in your career or ministry. Write it below.

⹈❈⹈

You want to be like Christ? Find the least desired position, the task no one else wants, the worst seat in the house, and claim it. Make it yours. —*So, You Want to Be Like Christ?*

God doesn't want you merely to *act* humble, but to *be* humble. Yet true humility will result in actions, and humble actions will nurture true humility. The discipline of humility is grounded in your spiritual security in Christ and in an intimate relationship with Him. It's also built upon a realistic understanding of your gifts, training, and skills accompanied by contentment with your God-designed purpose in life, however lowly or exalted. Following the example of Christ, you can exercise humility through actions that put the needs of others above your own.

Self-Control:
Holding Back

Self-Control:
Holding Back

THE HEART OF THE MATTER

Every one of us engages in battle with "the flesh"—that self–serving, nonbelieving, and godless drive within us. Yet the Spirit of God dwells in believers, waging war against the flesh and shaping us more and more into the image of God's Son. The discipline of self-control is really "Spirit-control," as we allow the Spirit to conquer the flesh and usher us into a deeper, more intimate relationship with God. Along with this lesson, read chapter 7 of *So, You Want to Be Like Christ?*

YOU ARE HERE . . .

The apostle Paul was an undisputed spiritual giant, called upon by God to write God-breathed words and lead innumerable believers on the journey to Christlikeness. Yet Paul, like each one of us, found himself locked in mortal combat with the flesh—an evil disposition driven by a selfish, faithless, and godless mind-set whose natural stance is facing away from God. It was a battle Paul knew he could never win on his own.

Leader Help

By the end of this lesson, group members should recognize that struggles against sin are an ongoing, universal problem, but the indwelling Spirit provides power for victory over sin. Armed with an awareness of the Holy Spirit's power, they should also prepare themselves to face sin and walk in righteousness with confidence.

Leader Help

Set aside a few minutes at the beginning of this session to review the issue of humility from the previous lesson. Instead of sharing personal accomplishments in humility, group members may share how they've seen others demonstrate Christlike humility toward them.

Leader Help

The issue of self-control related to sin can be very personal. Individuals struggle with many, varying sins that have caused frustration, guilt, and shame. Encourage group members to share only what they are comfortable revealing.

Leader Help

Write group members' words on a board and allow several members to explain why they summarized the passage with these words. This will add insight into the significance of this passage to different people.

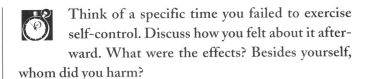 Think of a specific time you failed to exercise self-control. Discuss how you felt about it afterward. What were the effects? Besides yourself, whom did you harm?

 Read Romans 7:14–24 aloud. As challenging as this may be, try to summarize the passage in one or two key words that illustrate your reactions, emotions, or thoughts concerning Paul's struggle. (Modern translations like the NIV will likely make this easier.)

 Explain why you selected these words. Your reasons could be based on the passage or on issues in your own life experience or both.

According to Paul, what is the archenemy of walking in the Spirit?

In which of the following areas do you struggle with controlling the flesh? (Circle one answer for each.)

Losing temper	Never	Sometimes	Often
Overeating	Never	Sometimes	Often
Bad habits or addictions	Never	Sometimes	Often
Working too much	Never	Sometimes	Often
Procrastination	Never	Sometimes	Often
Worry	Never	Sometimes	Often
Other:_____	Never	Sometimes	Often

In which area do you think you need the most self-control?

Would those closest to you agree with your answers above?

We are in the middle of an inescapable fight, and I would suggest that most people fight it in the shadows, out of sight, and feeling all alone. No wonder so many of us feel defeated by sin and seriously consider giving up. —*So, You Want to Be Like Christ?*

Have you ever tried to break a bad habit or to enforce a good one? If so, what was it?

What did you do to break or enforce the habit?

GETTING TO THE ROOT
The Flesh

The Greek word *sárx*, "flesh," has a wide range of meanings—some positive and some negative. Positively, it can mean simply the physical body (Acts 2:31), humanity in general (John 1:14), or all living creatures (1 Peter 1:24). As part of God's creation, "flesh" in this sense is good. However, Paul most often uses the term in a technical sense for the sinful disposition of humanity after the Fall and our inability to always obey in our own strength (Romans 7:18). "Everything human and earthly is *sárx*, and as people trust in *sárx* in this sense, it becomes a power that opposes the working of the Spirit. . . . Subjection to *sárx* is not fate but guilt. A life oriented to *sárx* serves it and carries out its thinking."[1]

DISCOVERING THE WAY . . .

Paul's raw honesty about the flesh in Romans 7:14–24 should hit each one of us hard. Man or woman, child or grandparent, pastor or president—nobody is immune. Why? Because the effect of the Fall on our corruptible flesh pervades humanity. That's all of us. None of us is exempt. Yet the Bible follows up its brutal description of our present condition with a message of confidence, hope, and even thanksgiving: "Thanks be to God through Jesus Christ our Lord!" (Romans 7:25). Thankfully, the believer in Jesus Christ has the Spirit of God living in him or her. The Spirit's regenerative work from the inside out can free us from slavish obedience to the flesh. In reality, the discipline often called "self-control" is "Spirit-control."

It is obvious what kind of life develops out of trying to get your own way all the time: repetitive, loveless, cheap sex; a stinking accumulation of mental and emotional garbage; frenzied and joyless grabs for happiness; trinket gods; magic-show religion; para-noid loneliness; cutthroat competition; all-consum-ing-yet-never-satisfied wants; a brutal temper; an impotence to love or be loved; divided homes and divided lives; small-minded and lopsided pursuits; the vicious habit of depersonalizing everyone into a rival; uncontrolled and uncontrollable addictions; ugly parodies of community. I could go on. (Galatians 5:17–21 MSG)

In the above paraphrase of Paul's description of the "deeds of the flesh," underline those things that might have special significance for you—things with which you have struggled personally or through which you've been harmed by another.

Our bodies are a precious gift from God, so they are by no means evil. But given the opportunity, our bodily drives will rule us. —*So, You Want to Be Like Christ?*

The conflict between the flesh and the indwelling Spirit is summed up by Paul in Galatians 5:17—"For the flesh sets its desire against the Spirit, and the Spirit against the flesh; for these are in opposition to one another, so that you may not do the things that you please." What was Paul's solution? He wrote, "But I say, walk by the Spirit, and you will not carry out the desire of the flesh" (Galatians 5:16). When we submit to the Spirit's leading and allow His power to conquer the flesh, the fruit of the Spirit will manifest itself. The "fruit" of the Spirit simply means the results of the Spirit's regenerating work in us. As the Spirit wins victories over the desire of the flesh, some of the following characteristics show up in our attitude and actions:

> But the fruit of the Spirit is love, joy, peace, patience, kindness, goodness, faithfulness, gentleness, self-control. (Galatians 5:22–23)

 In Paul's list of the fruit of the Spirit, circle the characteristics that you lack today.

Failure to exercise the discipline of self-control is an open invitation for Satan to rob us of all the good things we receive from God. —*So, You Want to Be Like Christ?*

 According to Galatians 5:22–23, from whom does "self-control" come?

Read 1 John 1:8–10. John makes it clear that those who say they have no sin have neither the truth nor God's Word in them. However, those of us who have the indwelling Holy Spirit know that our flesh wages war against us. Although this is a universal problem, your par-

ticular struggles are unique. What does 1 John 1:9 promise about your struggle against sin?

In 1 John 2:1, what is John's desire for believers?

In Romans 8, Paul describes the power of the Spirit that conquers the deeds of the flesh. Read Romans 8:5–8. What word repeated three times in verses 6 and 7 tells us what the flesh and Spirit fight to possess?

In Romans 8:9, who are those that are "in the Spirit"?

If we did not have the Spirit of Christ in us, what hope for success would we have against sin?

Leader Help

It is important for group members to be sure of their salvation, because the battle with sin cannot be won apart from a relationship with Christ and the presence of His indwelling Spirit. It may be helpful to review the gospel for the benefit of those who may have never heard it and to reassure believers of their security in Christ.

It is impossible for those who do not belong to Christ and do not have the Spirit to win the war against the flesh. If you are unsure about whether you belong to Christ, read "How to Begin a Relationship with God" on pages 139–142.

Read Romans 12:1–2. How can the mind ever hope to understand the good, acceptable, and perfect will of God?

❦

Now, if we can't win this fight, then Scripture is mocking us by dangling a hope that will never be realized. And to put it bluntly, Paul is a liar. But fortunately, we're in a winnable war. Paul isn't lying. — *So, You Want to Be Like Christ?*

In this battle, what is our responsibility (see Romans 12:1–2)?

Practically speaking, why do you think the mind is such an important battlefield (see James 1:4-16; Psalm 119:11; 2 Corinthians 10:5)?

STARTING YOUR JOURNEY . . .

We cannot hope to control the flesh on our own. That's a God-sized task that the Holy Spirit within us will accomplish. Our role is to submit to the Spirit, surrender to His leading, and allow Him to live His life through us. How do we do that? Being convinced of your need by the Spirit's prompting and being empowered by the Spirit to humble yourself under the hand of God, your life of self-control and victory over sin begins with a sincere commitment. You make a resolute decision of the mind to place your will into the hands of the only Person who can keep it under control.

Repent from relying on the flesh to conquer your habits, sins, and shortfalls, and commit to living a life of righteousness by God's power, not yours. Through prayer, surrender your will to God in humility, asking that the Spirit usher you in to a moment-by-moment, intimate reliance on God that empowers you to identify sources of temptation and either avoid or overcome them. Write a prayer to this effect in your own words:

Copy this prayer into your prayer journal or onto a small card and place it somewhere to remind you to recommit to this calling to live by the Spirit's power daily.

Identify the temptations and sins over which you have the least self-control. Use the words you underlined in your study of Galatians 5:17–21 on page 113 to get started. In what other thoughts and deeds has the flesh been winning battles in your life too often?

Place these specific issues on your prayer list or in your prayer journal. Each time you pray, turn these over to God, allowing Him to fight the battle.

 From the following questions, select one or two activities to help you live a lifestyle of self-control.

❏ Identify positive fruit of the Spirit that you desire God to cultivate in your life. Use the words you circled in your study of Galatians 5:22–23 on page 114 to get started. What other attitudes and actions of righteousness would you like to see manifested in your life?

Place these specific issues on your prayer list or in your prayer journal. Each time you pray, turn these over to God to cultivate them.

❏ Now that you have identified areas of sin that you will hand over to God to conquer, what's your next step? Make a game plan. Read 1 Corinthians 9:24–27. In what ways would you compare the preparation and training of an athlete for competition or a soldier for combat to a believer's preparation for the battle against sin? What steps of preparation can you take now that will prepare you for the moment of temptation? It's a good idea to discuss this issue with someone who may have once struggled as you do now.

❏ Read 1 Corinthians 10:13. Write it below. In Psalm 119:11, the psalmist armed himself against sin by meditating on God's Word and hiding it in his heart. Consider committing the verse you write below to memory as a way of reminding yourself of God's powerful presence even in the face of temptation.

❏ Reflect on your most common temptations or struggles with sin in which you lose control. Where does this most often happen? Who is involved? At what time of the day? What are the circumstances? As you examine this matter objectively, what "way of escape" is evident? What can you change in your life that will close the doors of opportunity for this kind of temptation and sin?

Let's get practical. I have found that a three-second pause can make all the difference. Just as an impulse hits me, I decide to wait just three seconds before taking any action. During that pause, I do a quick assessment of what the consequences might be. . . . Those three seconds have kept me out of a lot of hot water over the years. —*So, You Want to Be Like Christ?*

Leader Help

End this session in prayer, asking that the Holy Spirit convict you and your group of sin and remind each of you of Christ's provision for righteousness. Group members should be encouraged to work through this lesson carefully and prayerfully as the issues discussed in this lesson can mean the difference between victory or defeat in the Christian life.

Leader Help

The next lesson begins with an exercise that requires the group members to have advance notice. If you plan to use the suggestion, now may be a good time to tell the group members how to prepare.

To win the civil war raging within, you must know your enemy. Besides the world and the devil, the greatest enemy is your own flesh. If your life has been claimed by Christ, and the Spirit has invaded your whole being, the conflict with the flesh began that moment and continues to this day. Until the Lord returns and transforms your mortal body into one that cannot sin (Romans 8:11), you will struggle against its desires. That's a good sign! It's a sign of life! The only sign of defeat is when the battle between your flesh and His Spirit ceases. Thankfully, the Spirit will never retreat, so take heart! The victory is sure!

What's your role in the battle? To surrender your mind, your will, and your actions to God. By His grace He has already forgiven you, if you have trusted in Christ. And by His grace He will also produce the fruit of the Spirit in your life. So, you want to be like Christ? Trust Him to live His life of self-control through you by the indwelling Spirit.

Sacrifice:
Giving Over

Sacrifice:
Giving Over

THE HEART OF THE MATTER

The discipline of sacrifice stands at the heart of Christlikeness. God calls each believer to a life of sacrifice first to God through faith and obedience, then to each other as we express our love through sacrificial giving of ourselves to meet the needs of others. Intimacy with God begins and ends with self-less attitudes and actions that require constant devotion to being like Christ. Along with this lesson, read chapter 8 of *So, You Want to Be Like Christ?*

YOU ARE HERE ...

Of the spiritual disciplines, sacrifice may be the most Christlike. The Crucifixion—as both the climax of His mission and the center of the gospel message—focuses on the sacrifice of His life for us: "For even the Son of Man did not come to be served, but to serve, and to give His life a ransom for many" (Mark 10:45). You may recall that in our key passage on intimacy with God, Philippians 3:10, Paul expressed his desire to know "the fellowship of His sufferings, being conformed to His death."

Leader Help

By the end of this lesson, group members should acknowledge that true Christlikeness will express itself through a life of daily sacrifice motivated by love, and they should cultivate a sacrificial attitude by engaging in specific acts of selflessness.

Leader Help

Before beginning this lesson, group members should share their personal experiences with the discipline of self-control since the last meeting. Encourage some to share not only victories, but also frustrations. Be prepared to offer your own example.

Although God will occasionally ask believers to suffer martyrdom for the sake of Christ, the sacrifice He wants from all of us and the one to which Paul referred is a *living* sacrifice. When we get out of bed in the morning, as we arrive at work and put in those hours, as we relate to others, as we play, as we carry out our personal responsibilities, as we fall into bed at night, we are to do everything as a deliberate act of submission and obedience to God. That path leads to our becoming a living, breathing sacrifice—dead to anything our Master hates, alive to everything He loves.

Leader Help

As part of this warmup, you may ask group members to exchange an inexpensive, white-elephant gift at this final meeting. Or discuss how members would feel if they discovered that a romantic gift had been given to them secondhand. Discuss why gifts given without sacrifice are unsatisfying.

 What is the most memorable and special gift you've ever received?

 Did the giver sacrifice to give it?

 Think of a gift you have given that you would describe as sacrificial. What made this gift a sacrifice?

What motivated you to give it?

 How did you feel while (or after) giving this gift?

Yes, He was intimate with the Father, lived simply, sought solitude, surrendered His will to the Father daily, and lived a prayerful, humble life characterized by self-control. But it is sacrifice that distinguishes the Son of God from all mere historical figures and identifies Him as Savior—even to those who scarcely know of Him. — *So, You Want to Be Like Christ?*

 ## DISCOVERING THE WAY . . .

The discipline of sacrifice begins with a choice. Who or what should we trust to meet our needs and desires? We naturally serve what we trust. Hoarding wealth is a sure sign that a person trusts his or her things instead of God. Personal sacrifice overcomes a love for self that may be nurtured by any number of things, material wealth being only one of them. The apostle Paul knew how to model the sacrifice of Christ in his daily life. We would do well to listen to his words:

[1]Therefore I urge you, brethren, by the mercies of God, to present your bodies a living and holy sacrifice, acceptable to God, which is your spiritual service of worship. [2]And do not be conformed to this world, but be transformed by the renewing of your mind, so that you may prove what the will of God is, that which is good and acceptable and perfect. (Romans 12:1–2)

In Romans 12:1, underline the phrase that describes what Paul urged his readers to do. What should motivate this act according to the verse?

 What two commands—one negative and one positive—do you see in Romans 12:2? Write them here:

but

 What is the ultimate purpose for doing these things, according to the end of Romans 12:2?

 Why do you think becoming a living sacrifice and being transformed in our minds are necessary in order to have the ability to discern God's will?

What does Paul mean by "renewing" the mind? The Greek word translated "renewal" is *anakainō-sis* and the verb form is *anakainizō*. A study of Paul's other uses of these and similar words will help us better understand what Paul meant by renewing the mind. Look up the following passages, and note what they teach about renewal.

2 Corinthians 4:16

Ephesians 4:22–24

Colossians 3:9–10

How does renewing your mind relate to being a living sacrifice?

 Compare Romans 12:1–2 with Romans 6:12–13. What thoughts or phrases do you see that are similar?

Leader Help

Members can break up into three groups for two minutes, then have each group briefly share their answers based on these passages. Or have three members share their answers from previous preparation and then discuss these answers in the group for a few minutes.

Sacrifice hurts. Sacrifice works against our natural inclinations to keep a tight hold on our possessions and creature comforts. And we come hard-wired with the instinct to watch out for ourselves, guard against risk, and preserve our own lives at any cost. —*So, You Want to Be Like Christ?*

 According to your detailed study of Romans 12:1–2, what do you sense God is leading you to do?

DIGGING DEEPER

 The Mercies of God
What are the "mercies of God"? In Romans 3 Paul described the mercy of *justification*—the act of wiping out the sin and guilt of those who simply trust in Christ for salvation. In Romans 5 he began a discussion of *sanctification*—the act of the Spirit empowering believers to overcome sin and resist temptation in this life. In Romans 8 Paul addressed the issue of *glorification*—the final experience of salvation in which believers are glorified in new bodies, finally victorious over sin and death. These past, present, and future experiences of salvation are regarded by Paul as "the mercies of God." Everything he described in these passages should be a motivation for believers to offer themselves completely to God's service. Paul offered his readers a description of his own experience of God's mercy:

> I thank Christ Jesus our Lord, who has strengthened me, because He considered me faithful, putting me into service, even though I was formerly a blasphemer and a persecutor and a violent aggressor. Yet I was shown mercy because I acted ignorantly in unbelief; and the grace of our Lord was more than abundant, with the faith and love which are found in Christ Jesus. (1 Timothy 1:12–14)

Each of us has our own story of experiencing God's mercies as we contrast what our life was and would have been without Christ with the blessings He has given us in our relationship with Him.

———————————————————

Paul urged us to live sacrificial lives for God because of His "mercies." How would you summarize the mercies of God in the following passages?

Romans 5:6–8

Titus 3:4–7

1 Peter 2:9–10

Jude 21

Which of these examples of God's mercy produces the greatest sense of gratitude in you? Give a specific example from your personal experience.

In light of Paul's words, how would a deep sense of gratitude influence your desire to live sacrificially or selflessly?

*An offering is a sacrifice with an added element: choice. To sacrifice is to give up something for the sake of something else that is much better. An offering is a voluntary act. Christ made a conscious choice to offer Himself as an atoning sacrifice so that He might have us. We are to make that same choice for the sake of having Him in a more intimate way.
—So, You Want to Be Like Christ?*

Read John 15:13–17. In verse 13, how is love demonstrated?

Compare verses 13 and 14. How did Christ demonstrate His intimate friendship with the disciples?

How were the disciples to demonstrate their intimate friendship with Christ?

In verse 15, in what specific way did the relationship between Christ and His disciples differ from that of a master and slave or employer and employee?

Based on verses 16 and 17, describe how you see this intimate relationship with Christ expressing itself toward those inside and outside the fellowship of believers. What role does sacrifice play in this?

John 3:16 describes the ultimate expression of sacrificial love. Have you experienced this love of God? If not, or if you're unsure, you may wish to read "How to Begin a Relationship with God" on pages 139–142.

STARTING YOUR JOURNEY...

God patiently waits for us to sacrifice ourselves in small amounts, one decision at a time, one day at a time, so that we might enjoy an ever-increasing intimacy with Him. Sacrifice is an act of love, an act supremely illustrated when God sent His only Son to become man and to die for our sins (John 3:16). This self-sacrificing love manifests itself through us when we surrender our wills to God, who transforms our minds through His Spirit to conform us to the image of His Son. When our hearts learn to love selflessly as He does, we will naturally display the love of Christ toward others.

Yet we must be willing to give God our very best, to put to death our self-interest and personal wills. God doesn't want our grubby secondhand gifts. He wants our most priceless treasure—those relationships, those possessions, those positions we are most afraid to lay aside. Why? Because our love is directed there. The most precious sacrifice to God is the one that is the most costly to self. Do you want to be like Christ? Sacrifice as He did.

 The world urges us to do all sorts of things for ourselves. Paul urges us to live sacrificially, doing all things for Christ and manifesting our love for Him by loving others. In the following table, note various examples of ways the world tells us to seek after our own interests. Then, in the second column, think of alternative actions that would express sacrificial love for Christ and others.

Leader Help

This exercise contrasts the influences of the world to which we are easily conformed with acts of sacrifice that do not fit the world's pattern. You may want to reproduce these two contrasting columns on a marker board and brainstorm ideas with your group. Focus attention on the second column and ideas for specific acts of loving sacrifice for God and others.

The World's Pattern of Self-Seeking Action	Christ's Pattern of Self-Sacrificial Action

Consider some of the adversaries or obstacles in the world that would challenge your intention to sacrifice something of value (time, talents, resources) for the purpose of cultivating spiritual intimacy with God.

Leader Help

In preparation for this discussion, see some of the challenges under the heading "Warnings" in chapter 8 of *So, You Want to Be Like Christ?* Group members should think of specific examples of obstacles they may encounter as they consider sacrificing in such areas as their time, talents, and resources.

The life of sacrifice must begin with the mind. This means making a decision to turn your will over to God and instead allow His will to be done through the Holy Spirit working in you. You can't do this on your own. Take a moment to literally "present your bod[y] a living and holy sacrifice" to God through prayer.

Select a specific activity of sacrificial living from the following suggestions, or come up with your own. Commit to doing it this week. Write your choice in the following space.

❏ Save the money you would spend going out for dinner for one or two meals and give it to your church or to a particular ministry. By making this a regular practice in your family, you will have ample opportunities to teach your children the importance of sacrificial giving.

❑ Reexamine your schedule (you may use the "time budget" exercise you did in lesson 2 on simplicity). Are there any items that now appear to you to be self-serving and excessive that you could give up for the greater good of someone else? Don't just give up an activity without a strategy for using that time to meet another person's needs.

❑ If your life seems caught up in a cycle of me-ism and self-indulgence, consider fasting as a way of sacrificing your own pleasures for the greater good of focusing on God. Think about how much time, attention, and energy you put into planning and enjoying a meal. What would happen if you redirected your energies toward God rather than toward yourself during that time? Choosing to give up the temporal enjoyment of a meal as an expression of worship can help you reorder your priorities and humble yourself before God. (Isaiah 58 is a helpful passage regarding fasting.)

❑ Consider using your next vacation to participate in a short-term mission trip or to minister locally to a very needy people or place.

May I press the point? When was the last time you just gave something away? I mean something very nice. Something that has meant something to you? It won't be easy. Sacrifice doesn't come naturally. It's a discipline that requires faith—a trust that the Almighty will look after your needs in ways that you will never see until you allow Him the opportunity. —*So, You Want to Be Like Christ?*

The discipline of sacrifice is one in which we forsake the security of meeting our needs with what is in our hands. It is total abandonment to God, a stepping into the darkened abyss in the faith and hope that God will bear us up. . . .

The cautious faith that never saws off a limb on which it is sitting never learns that unattached limbs may find strange, unaccountable ways of not falling.[1] —Dallas Willard

❑ Read Acts 2:44–45. How did early believers sacrifice for each other? Compare the practice of the first church with your own practice of giving. In what ways is it similar? In what ways is it different? Now, consider the needs of your friends and relatives. Some of these needs might be unexpressed. If you are married, discuss this with your spouse. Do you have anything that would help meet that person's needs? This does not necessarily need to be a financial help, but could be time, a particular possession, or something else. How can you sacrificially meet that person's need?

❑ Read the example of self-sacrificial love of a husband toward his wife in Ephesians 5:22–33. Husbands, think of specific, meaningful, self-sacrificial acts that express your love for your wives; then do them regularly. Wives, what can you do to sacrificially express respect and honor to your husband?

GRAY MATTERS
Materialism versus Asceticism

Christians throughout history have had a tendency to go to unhealthy extremes that distort the biblical model of a balanced, Spirit-led Christian life. Just think about all the different approaches out there to material possessions and entertainment.

Materialism stands at one extreme. Characterized by unbridled accumulation of possessions and uncontrolled indulgence in worldly things, this pursuit crowns selfishness as king. Sacrifice is never even considered.

Asceticism stands at the other extreme. Described as an extreme self-denial of worldly goods and of physical or mental enjoyment, this approach advocates that everything be sacrificed for the sake of personal and spiritual gain.

Christians should regard both materialism and asceticism as unacceptable extremes. But where does the proper balance lie? Take some time to discuss or think through how Christians should approach questions of entertainment, possessions, and leisure and the extremes that believers often take in these areas. Use the following questions and scriptures as a guide:

- Is it ever wrong to live a lifestyle that includes luxury cars, homes, travel, and entertainment? If so, how much is too much?

- How much of one's income should go toward charitable causes?

- Defend this statement: "Asceticism is just as self-centered as materialism."

Leader Help

At the close of this lesson, group members may take some time to discuss the relationship between all of the disciplines—intimacy, simplicity, silence and solitude, surrender, prayer, humility, self-control, and sacrifice. How do they fit together as we seek to model the life of Christ? Discuss how the exercises in this workbook have contributed to spiritual intimacy. Group members may also discuss their trials, struggles, frustrations, and concerns about some of the issues brought up through this study. Encourage members in the practice of the disciplines as a lifelong process and remind them that the reward of practicing them is intimacy with God. Close in prayer, consecrating the group to God as living sacrifices, holy and acceptable to Him.

- According to the following passages, what should be the Christian's attitude toward materialism and asceticism?

  Ecclesiastes 2:1–11
  Ecclesiastes 5:18–19
  Matthew 11:18–19
  1 John 2:15–17
  1 Timothy 4:1–5
  1 Timothy 6:17–19

To be like Christ is to be a living sacrifice. All of the spiritual disciplines addressed in this study relate to intimacy and to sacrifice. By intimacy we relate to God through Christ in the power of the Holy Spirit. By a life of sacrifice we demonstrate our relationship to God in our love toward others. God has called all those who know Him intimately to a life of sacrifice, first to God through faith and obedience, then to each other as we express our love through sacrificial giving of our time, resources, gifts, and abilities to meet the needs of others. Intimacy with God begins and ends with sacrificial attitudes and actions. So, you want to be like Christ? Offer your life to God as a living sacrifice.

How to Begin a Relationship with God

Christlikeness is not a system of religious practices, a lifestyle of personal morality, or a rigid adherence to particular doctrines or principles. Christlikeness begins with a relationship. Apart from a real, spiritual, and eternal relationship with God, the exercise of spiritual disciplines will be dissatisfying for us and displeasing to God. Yet if intimacy with the Almighty is the key, how can we come to know Him? In a world filled with competing religions, all claiming to have the better way, can we know for sure that our relationship with God is genuine?

The most marvelous book in the world, the Bible, marks the path to God with four vital truths. Let's look at each marker in detail.

1. Our Spiritual Condition: Totally Depraved

The first truth is rather personal. One look in the mirror of Scripture, and our human condition becomes painfully clear:

> There is none righteous, not even one;
> There is none who understands,
> There is none who seeks for God;
> All have turned aside, together they have become useless;
> There is none who does good,
> There is not even one. (Romans 3:10–12)

We are all sinners through and through—totally depraved. Now, that doesn't mean we've committed every atrocity known to humankind. We're not as *bad* as we can be, just as *bad off* as we can be. Sin colors all our thoughts, motives, words, and actions.

You still don't believe it? Look around. Everything around us bears the smudge marks of our sinful nature. Despite our best efforts to create a perfect world, crime statistics continue to soar, divorce rates keep climbing, and families keep crumbling.

Something has gone terribly wrong in our society and in ourselves, something deadly. Contrary to how the world would repackage it, me-first living doesn't equal rugged individuality and freedom; it equals death. As Paul said in his letter to the Romans, "The wages of sin is death" (6:23)—our emotional and physical death through sin's destructiveness and our spiritual death from God's righteous judgment of our sin. This brings us to the second marker: God's character.

2. God's Character: Infinitely Holy

When he observed the condition of the world and the people in it, the wise King Solomon concluded, "Vanity of vanities, all is vanity" (Ecclesiastes 1:2; 12:8). The fact that we know things are not as they should be points us to a standard of goodness beyond ourselves. Our sense of injustice in life "under the sun" implies a perfect standard of justice "above the sun." That standard and source is God Himself. And God's standard of holiness contrasts starkly with our sinful condition.

Scripture says that "God is light, and in Him there is no darkness at all" (1 John 1:5). He is absolutely holy, which creates a problem for us. If God is so pure, how can we who are so impure relate to Him?

Perhaps we could try being better people, try to tilt the balance in favor of our good deeds, or seek out wisdom and knowledge for self-improvement. Throughout history, people have attempted to live up to God's standard by keeping the Ten Commandments or living by their own code of ethics. Unfortunately, no one can come close to satisfying the demands of God's law. Romans 3:20 says, "By the works of the Law no flesh will be justified in His sight; for through the Law comes the knowledge of sin."

3. Our Need: A Substitute

So here we are, sinners by nature, sinners by choice, trying to pull ourselves up by our own bootstraps and attain a relationship with our holy Creator. But every time we try, we fall flat on our faces. We can't live a good enough life to make up for our sin, because God's standard isn't "good enough"; it's perfection. And we can't make amends for the offense our sin has created without dying for it.

Who can get us out of this mess?

If someone could live perfectly, honoring God's law, and would bear sin's death penalty for us—in our place—then we would be saved from our predicament. But is there such a person? Thankfully, yes!

Meet your substitute—*Jesus Christ*. He is the One who took death's place for you!

> [God] made [Jesus Christ] who knew no sin to be sin on our behalf, that we might become the righteousness of God in Him. (2 Corinthians 5:21)

4. God's Provision: A Savior

God rescued us by sending His Son, Jesus, to die for our sins on the cross (see 1 John 4:9–10). Jesus was fully human and fully divine (see John 1:1, 18), a truth that ensures His understanding of our weaknesses, His power to forgive, and His ability to bridge the gap between God and us (see Romans 5:6–11). In short, we are "justified as a gift by His grace through the redemption which is in Christ Jesus" (Romans 3:24). Two words in this verse bear further explanation: *justified* and *redemption*.

Justification is God's act of mercy, in which He declares believing sinners righteous, while they are still in their sinning state. Justification doesn't mean that God *makes* us righteous, so that we never sin again, rather that He *declares* us righteous—much as a judge pardons a guilty criminal. Because Jesus took our sin upon Himself and suffered our judgment on the cross, God forgives our debt and proclaims us *pardoned*.

Redemption is God's act of paying the ransom price to release us from our bondage to sin. Held hostage by Satan, we were shackled by the iron chains of sin and death. Like a loving parent whose child has been kidnapped, God willingly paid the ransom for you. And what a price He paid! He gave His only Son to bear our sins—past, present, and future. Jesus's death and resurrection broke our chains and set us free to become children of God (see Romans 6:16–18, 22; Galatians 4:4–7).

Placing Your Faith in Christ

These four truths describe how God has provided a way to Himself through Jesus Christ. Since the price has been paid in full by God, we must respond to His free gift of eternal life in total faith and confidence in Him to save us. We must step forward into the relationship with God that He has prepared for us—not by doing good works or being a good person, but by coming to Him just as we are and accepting His justification and redemption by faith.

For by grace you have been saved through faith; and that not of yourselves, it is the gift of God; not as a result of works, that no one should boast. (Ephesians 2:8–9)

We accept God's gift of salvation simply by placing our faith in Christ alone for the forgiveness of our sins. Would you like to enter a relationship with your Creator by trusting in Christ as your Savior? If so, here's a simple prayer you can use to express your faith:

> *Dear God,*
>
> *I know that my sin has put a barrier between You and me. Thank You for sending Your Son, Jesus, to die in my place. I trust in Jesus alone to forgive my sins, and I accept His gift of eternal life. I ask Jesus to be my personal Savior and the Lord of my life. Thank You. In Jesus's name, amen.*

If you've prayed this prayer or one like it, and you wish to find out more about knowing God and His plan for you in the Bible, contact us at Insight for Living. You can speak to one of our pastors on staff by calling (972) 473-5097. Or you can write to us at the address below. Mark your letter to the Pastoral Ministries Department.

Of all the relationships you enjoy in this life, none can compare with a relationship with God through Jesus Christ, who loved us and gave Himself for us. So, you want to be like Christ? Begin with an intimate, personal, and eternal relationship with God.

Pastoral Ministries Department
Insight for Living
PO Box 269000
Plano, Texas 75026-9000

Notes

Lesson 1

Unless otherwise noted below, all material is adapted or quoted from Charles R. Swindoll, *So, You Want to Be Like Christ? Eight Essentials to Get You There* (Nashville: W Publishing Group, 2005).

1. Richard J. Foster, *Celebration of Discipline: The Path to Spiritual Growth* (San Francisco: Harper & Row, 1978), 1.
2. Homer A. Kent, Jr., "Philippians," in *The Expositor's Bible Commentary*, vol. 11, Ephesians—Philemon, ed. Frank E. Gaebelein and others (Grand Rapids, Mich.: Zondervan Publishing House, 1978), 140–41.
3. Kenneth Wuest, *Wuest's Word Studies from the Greek New Testament,* vol. 2 (Grand Rapids, Mich.: William B. Eerdmans Publishing Company, 1973; reprint, 2002), 70.

Lesson 2

1. Thomas à Kempis, *The Imitation of Christ* (Milwaukee: The Bruce Publishing Company, 1940), 59.
2. Gerhard Kittel, Gerhard Friedrich, and Geoffrey W. Bromiley, eds., *Theological Dictionary of the New Testament,* abridged ed. (Grand Rapids, Mich.: William B. Eerdmans Publishing Company, 1985), 65.

Lesson 3

1. Walter Bauer and others, eds., *A Greek-English Lexicon of the New Testament and Other Early Christian Literature,* 2d rev. ed. (Chicago: University of Chicago Press, 1979), 309.

Lesson 4

1. Judson W. VanDeVenter, "I Surrender All," in *The Hymnal for Worship and Celebration* (Waco, Tex.: Word Music, 1986), no. 366.

2. For a scholarly discussion of these different views, see Gordon D. Fee, ed. *Paul's Letter to the Philippians,* The New International Commentary on the New Testament (Grand Rapids, Mich.: William B. Eerdmans Publishing Company, 1995), 205–207.

Lesson 5

1. Dallas Willard, *The Spirit of the Disciplines: Understanding How God Changes Lives* (San Francisco: Harper & Row, 1988), 185.

Lesson 6

1. Thomas à Kempis, *The Imitation of Christ* (Milwaukee: The Bruce Publishing Company, 1940), 10.

Lesson 7

1. Gerhard Kittel, Gerhard Friedrich, and Geoffrey W. Bromiley, eds., *Theological Dictionary of the New Testament,* abridged ed. (Grand Rapids, Mich.: William B. Eerdmans Publishing Company, 1985), 1005.

Lesson 8

1. Dallas Willard, *The Spirit of the Disciplines: Understanding How God Changes Lives* (San Francisco: Harper & Row, 1988), 175.